Minilessons for Math Practice

GRADES 3-5

Minilessons for Math Practice

GRADES 3-5

Rusty Bresser

Caren Holtzman

Math Solutions
Sausalito, California, USA

Math Solutions
One Harbor Drive, Suite 101
Sausalito, CA 94965
www.mathsolutions.com

Library of Congress Cataloging-in-Publication Data
Bresser, Rusty.
   Minilessons for math practice : grades 3–5 / Rusty Bresser, Caren Holtzman.
      p. cm.
   Includes bibliographical references and index.
   ISBN-13: 978-0-941355-75-9 (alk. paper)
   ISBN-10: 0-941355-75-6
   1. Mathematics—Problems, exercises, etc.—Juvenile literature. 2. Mathematics—Study
and teaching (Elementary)—Juvenile literature. 3. Problem solving—Study and teaching
(Elementary)—Juvenile literature. I. Holtzman, Caren, II. Title.
   QA43.B729 2006
   372.7—dc22
                                                                              2006017050

Editor: Toby Gordon
Production: Melissa L. Inglis
Cover design: Jan Streitburger
Interior design: Catherine Hawkes/Cat & Mouse
Composition: Interactive Composition Corporation

Printed in the United States of America on acid-free paper
15 14 13 12   AAP   7 8 9 10

A Message from Math Solutions

We at Math Solutions believe that teaching math well calls for increasing our understanding of the math we teach, seeking deeper insights into how students learn mathematics, and refining our lessons to best promote students' learning.

Math Solutions shares classroom-tested lessons and teaching expertise from our faculty of professional development consultants as well as from other respected math educators. Our publications are part of the nationwide effort we've made since 1984 that now includes

- more than five hundred face-to-face professional development programs each year for teachers and administrators in districts across the country;

- professional development books that span all math topics taught in kindergarten through high school;

- videos for teachers and for parents that show math lessons taught in actual classrooms;

- on-site visits to schools to help refine teaching strategies and assess student learning; and

- free online support, including grade-level lessons, book reviews, inservice information, and district feedback, all in our Math Solutions Online Newsletter.

For information about all of the products and services we have available, please visit our website at *www.mathsolutions.com.* You can also contact us to discuss math professional development needs by calling (800) 868-9092 or by sending an email to *info@mathsolutions.com.*

We're always eager for your feedback and interested in learning about your particular needs. We look forward to hearing from you.

Contents

Acknowledgments

We thank the following people for making this book possible: Marilyn Burns, for her guidance and support; Toby Gordon and Maryann Wickett, for their editorial expertise; and Melissa L. Inglis, for her work on the book's production.

Our sincerest appreciation to the educators and administrators who opened their classrooms to us: from Florence Elementary School, San Diego, CA: Principal Mary Estill, Olivia Gonzalez, Robin Gordon, Amy Jackson, and Lisa Kimbrell; from Freese Elementary School, San Diego, CA: Principal Midge Backensto, Melissa Mechtly, Danielle Pickett, and Patty Starks; from Jackson Elementary School, San Diego, CA: Principal Rupi Boyd and Tina Rasori.

Introduction: Redefining Practice

Teachers have always known that their students require opportunities to practice the things they have learned. Opportunities for practice are particularly important in mathematics. When children learn a new skill or concept in math without having had the time to put that new idea into practice, they tend to forget what they've learned.

Traditionally, practice has been synonymous with drill. The teacher models or introduces a procedure or math fact and then gives students worksheets full of problems so that they can "practice" over and over. The objective of this form of practice has often been memorization rather than understanding.

The purpose of *Minilessons for Math Practice, Grades 3–5* is to broaden the notion of what it means to provide students with practice in mathematics. Instead of focusing just on facts, procedures, and memorization, the goal of this book is to give students ongoing experiences that will help them practice math concepts, skills, and processes so that they may deepen their understanding of mathematics and apply what they've learned to new problem situations.

Another goal of the book involves broadening classroom opportunities to do mathematics. There is limited time in the school day dedicated solely to math. This book looks at ways to insert mathematics throughout the students' day. *Minilessons for Math Practice* offers ideas for quick activities that can be used in various contexts.

In addition, a goal of this book is to broaden the mathematics curriculum. Most teachers are required to use a district-adopted curriculum and have little extra time for supplemental materials. The activities in this book can be used with any existing math program to help students meet local, state, and national math standards.

Features of This Book

There are several key features in *Minilessons for Math Practice*. One is that the activities in it take little or no preparation. They are easy to implement. And the activities take only five to fifteen minutes to teach. Throughout the day teachers find themselves transitioning their students from one activity to another, from one place to another, or from one subject to another. These transitional times require teachers to focus the attention of their students so they can move smoothly through shifts in the day. The activities in this book convert these transitional times into rich mathematical events.

Another important feature is that all of the activities can be repeated. For example, many of the games in the book can be played throughout the year to give students ongoing practice with numbers and operations. *Looking at Data* can be repeated simply by changing the survey question so that students can continue to practice analyzing data as the year progresses. For *Guess My Rule*, you need only to offer students different numbers to compare. Or you might shift the *Guess My Rule* content area by presenting polygons, in order to give students continued experience with two-dimensional shapes, even after your unit on geometry is over.

The lessons in *Minilessons for Math Practice* focus on questioning and classroom discussion. While the activities in the book are engaging and fun, they become mathematically loaded when the teacher spotlights the key mathematical concepts and skills. This spotlight becomes a focal point for the students when the teacher asks challenging questions and helps students develop their own ways to express their thinking using mathematical language.

Organization of the Activities

The twenty-seven activities in this book offer experiences in all of the content areas important to mathematics: number, measurement, geometry, data analysis and probability, and algebra. As well, the lessons model how to develop several important math processes: problem solving, reasoning and proof, communication, connections, and representation.

See the contents chart following this introduction to identify activities that fit the content area of choice. Since many of the activities address more than one content area, the content area of focus for each vignette is highlighted in the chart with a bold **X**. Other potential content connections are noted with a small x.

The activities in the book each have eight components:

1. the content area(s)
2. materials
3. time
4. an overview of the activity and an explanation of the mathematics involved
5. step-by-step teaching directions
6. a list of key questions to ask students during the lesson
7. a brief vignette from the classroom that describes how we taught the activity
8. ideas for extending the activity throughout the year

Getting Started

The activities provided in this book have been field-tested in diverse classroom settings. They typically take fifteen minutes or less. However, when introducing the activities to your students, you might find you need more time. In some cases it makes sense to budget a thirty- to forty-five-minute time slot for the first presentation of an activity. Much of the decision will depend on your students' prior experience and your goals for the session. Once you've made the initial time investment, the activities should run smoothly in a five- to fifteen-minute time slot for the rest of the year.

The lessons in *Minilessons for Math Practice* are language rich, allowing students to develop, organize, and explain their thinking. However, the ability to communicate mathematical ideas is a skill that develops over time. Your initial discussions with your students might be briefer and less profound than you had anticipated. Don't be discouraged. Over time, with good questions and a safe environment, students will become more confident and more competent in discussing their mathematical thinking. This is especially true for English language learners.

The key questions listed before each vignette and the descriptions of classroom interactions within the vignette give examples of activity structures that maximize participation and develop mathematical thinking and language. Notice that we use different types of questions throughout the activities. Some questions focus students on specific solutions, while other questions focus students on multiple approaches, strategies, or techniques.

Since the activities are designed primarily for whole-class settings, we gave special thought to meeting the needs of diverse learners. The activities need to be accessible to all students while also being rich enough to engage all students at deep mathematical levels. Throughout the book, the vignettes model ways to encourage participation by all students and ways to help students develop the language and communication skills necessary for math talk.

We encourage you to use the book flexibly and adapt the activities to best meet your instructional goals and your students' needs. You might use the activities to supplement your current unit of study in mathematics. Alternatively, you might use some activities in *Minilessons for Math Practice* to keep past math studies fresh in your students' minds. Another option is to use activities as previews or introductions to upcoming units of study.

We recognize that classroom teachers face more and more challenges each year as they struggle to help their students meet local, state, and national standards and perform well on standardized tests. We hope that the activities in this book will support you in these efforts and we encourage you to use the book in ways that best meet the needs of your students.

However you choose to use the book, we hope you find effective and fun ways to engage your students mathematically. We also hope this book helps open your students' minds to math throughout each day and throughout the school year.

Contents Chart

Activity	Chapter	Number and Operations	Algebra	Geometry	Measurement	Data Analysis and Probability
Number Talks	1	X				
Ballpark Estimation	2	X			x	
Clear the Board	3	X				
Coin Riddle	4	X		x		
Comparing Fractions	5	X				
Coordinate Tic-Tac-Toe	6		X			
Digit Place	7	X				
Dot Clusters	8	X		x		
Estimate and Measure	9	x			X	X
Estimation Jar	10	X				
Function Machine	11	x	X			
Guess My Number	12	X				
Guess My Rule	13	X		x		
How Far Away?	14	X				x
Looking at Data	15				x	X
Number Strings	16	X				
Odd Number Wins	17	X				
Over or Under	18	X			x	
Personal Numbers	19	X				
Race for Twenty	20		X			
Target 100/Target 0	21	X				
Tell Me All You Can	22	X				
Twenty Questions	23	X		x		
What Comes Next?	24		X			
What Page Are We On?	25	X				x
Whole-Class Pig	26	x				X
Your Choice Tic-Tac-Toe	27			X		

Number Talks

Overview

In this simple, yet powerful activity, students solve a computation problem presented by the teacher. After students solve the problem mentally, a class discussion ensues. The teacher asks questions and records students' thinking on the board. This activity fuels mathematical thinking and computational fluency.

Start with simple problems that students can solve fairly easily. The focus at the beginning is on helping students explain their thinking and communicate clearly. Both of these tasks are challenging, especially for English language learners. As students develop their communication skills, you can gradually present more challenging problems. The teacher's role during number talks is to help students clarify their thinking and connect their mathematical ideas to the appropriate symbols and notation. This means that teachers need to ask probing questions and translate informal discussions into formal mathematical vocabulary and notation. These teaching skills develop over time with practice. It's as important for teachers to practice number talks as it is for students.

Activity Directions

1. Write a computation problem horizontally on the board or an overhead transparency (e.g., $27 \times 2 =$).
2. Tell students to solve the problem mentally and pay attention to the way they solved it.
3. After a few moments, count aloud to three and have the students tell their answer in a whisper voice.
4. When the correct answer has been established, have individual students share their solution strategies.
5. Record students' strategies on the board using appropriate mathematical notation.

CONTENT AREA

Number and Operations

MATERIALS

- optional: overhead projector

TIME

ten minutes

Key Questions

- How did you solve the problem?
- Where did you start?
- Did anyone do it a different way?

From the Classroom

I started a number talk with Robin Gordon's fourth graders. As this was the first number talk I'd done with them, I decided to introduce a fairly simple equation. This way, we'd be able to focus on the communication aspect instead of getting too bogged down in the computation. After the students understood the focus and mechanics of the whole-class number talk, I planned to present them with more challenging problems to solve and discuss.

"OK," I told the students, "I'm going to write a problem on the overhead. Your job is to solve the problem mentally. What do I mean by that?"

"Do it in your head," Gregory responded.

"Right," I agreed. "You're going to look at the problem and then solve it mentally, in your brain. There are actually two things your brain will be doing. Not only are you going to solve the problem, but you're also going to pay attention to how you solved it so we can have a conversation about it."

"Oh," I added, "there's one more thing. When you think you know the answer, please don't shout it out. We want to make sure everyone has time to think and solve the problem without being interrupted or told the answer. OK?"

I looked seriously at the students to convey the importance of this rule. I waited for eye contact and nods. Then I wrote on the transparency:

$27 \times 2 =$

I gave the students a full thirty seconds to think about the problem. After a more than ample pause, I spoke to the class. "Thanks for controlling yourselves and not shouting out the answer," I complimented. "Thumbs up if you think you know the answer."

Everyone showed me an upturned thumb. Instead of having all the students vie to be the one to say the answer, I employed the choral response approach. That way everyone would get to share.

"Well, it looks like a lot of you have an answer. Here's what we're going to do," I explained. "I'm going to count to three. When I say, 'Three,' you're going to say the answer in a whisper voice. Ready? One. Two. Three."

To my surprise, I heard three or four different answers. I realized we needed to resolve that dispute before moving ahead with the number talk.

"Hmm," I told the class. "I heard several different answers. Take a minute or two to talk to your neighbors about what you think the answer is and why. Maybe that will help us agree on the correct answer."

I gave the students a few minutes to talk to each other. As they were discussing the problem, I prompted various groups with questions like "What do you think the answer is?" "Can you explain your thinking to your partners?" and "How can you prove that?" When I heard them reaching a consensus, I asked for their attention.

"OK," I said. "We'll try the same thing again. I'll count to three and you say the answer in a whisper voice. One. Two. Three."

"Fifty-four," the class responded in unison.

"Yes," I agreed. "Now for the interesting part. Who is willing to tell how you solved the problem?"

Many students raised their hands. I called on Jonquil.

"I pictured it vertically," she told us. "Twenty-seven plus twenty-seven."

"So you turned this multiplication problem into an addition problem. You knew twenty-seven times two is the same as twenty-seven plus twenty-seven. Like this?" I asked as I wrote on the overhead.

Jonquil

$$\begin{array}{r} 27 \\ +\ \ 27 \\ \hline \end{array}$$

"Yes," Jonquil replied. "And I did seven plus seven equals fourteen, so I wrote down the four and put the one on top of the two."

"Is this really a one?" I asked the class.

"No, it's a ten," Ricardo reminded us.

I am always a stickler about clarifying the value of digits when discussing arithmetic problems. Using proper terminology helps intermediate-grade students solidify their place-value foundations. Students often need to be reminded that face value is not necessarily place value. In this case, the one Jonquil carried was not really a one, but a ten.

"So what did you do with that ten?" I asked Jonquil.

"I added it to the two twenties. That made fifty and I already had the four, so it equaled fifty-four," she explained.

I recorded Jonquil's answer and asked if any students had thought of it differently. Many hands were raised. I called on Ricky.

"I split the twenty-seven into a twenty and a seven. Then I added the twenties and the sevens."

I wrote on the overhead:

Ricky

$$27 = 20 + 7$$
$$20 + 20 = 40$$
$$7 + 7 = 14$$
$$40 + 14 = 54$$

Raquel was the next to explain. She had a method similar to Ricky's but used multiplication instead of addition.

Raquel

$$27 = 20 + 7$$
$$7 \times 2 = 14$$
$$20 \times 2 = 40$$
$$40 + 14 = 54$$

I saw an opportunity to help students make some connections.

"Does Raquel's way remind you of anyone else's way?" I asked the class. There were many nods.

"Yeah, it's just like Ricky's," Andrea noticed.

"Except that Raquel timesed the numbers and Ricky plussed them," Laurence added.

"Yes," I replied, "Ricky and Raquel both broke the twenty-seven into a twenty and a seven, but Ricky used addition to solve the problem and Raquel used multiplication." Again, I took advantage of an occasion to gently reinforce proper mathematical terminology, replacing Laurence's words *timesed* and *plussed* with *multiplication* and *addition*.

"Who has a different way?" I asked again.

"Mine is like Jonquil's, but I used multiplication," Trudy told us.

"Tell us what you did," I prompted.

"I thought of it vertically, but I did twenty-seven times two instead of twenty-seven plus twenty-seven," she explained. "First I did two times seven, which is fourteen. I put down the four and carried the ten. Then I did two times twenty, which is forty, plus ten more is fifty."

Trudy had used the standard algorithm. I wrote on the overhead:

Trudy

$$\begin{array}{r} {\scriptstyle 1} \\ 27 \\ \times\ 2 \\ \hline 54 \end{array}$$

"Did anyone do it a different way?" I asked again. This time I called on Jonathan.

"I took the sevens out of the twenty-sevens so I just had twenty. Then I multiplied twenty times two and added back the sevens."

I recorded his method on the overhead as he talked me through it.

Jonathan

$20 \times 2 = 40$
$40 + 7 = 47$
$47 + 7 = 54$

"Wow," I remarked as I looked at the screen. "There are a lot of different mathematical ideas up here. Take a minute to look at all of these solutions. Then raise your hand if you have an idea that's not already up here." I gave the students some time to digest the methods already recorded. Janie raised her hand.

"I rounded the twenty-seven up to thirty because thirty is easy. Then I had to take away six."

"Where did the six come from?" I asked her.

"Because I added three to each twenty-seven to get it to thirty, so I had to take the two threes away," Janie explained.

I added her solution to the overhead transparency.

Janie

$27 + 3 = 30$
$30 \times 2 = 60$
$60 - 3 = 57$
$57 - 3 = 54$

"This is all very impressive," I commented to the class as I looked at the overhead transparency filled with their ideas. "You have a lot of ways to think about numbers and computation. That's really important for mathematicians. It's also really helpful when you can see how different methods have some of the same ideas in them. You did a nice job of making connections among your ideas."

I thanked the students for their attention and told them I would save the transparency for us to revisit and add to in the future. The students exhibited flexible thinking and good communication. I knew that these features of their math learning would continue to improve as they regularly engaged in number talks.

Extending the Activity

As students gain skill in communicating and connecting their ideas to mathematical symbols, they can take on the task of recording their own and each other's thinking. Number talks benefit students in all areas of number and operations. Regular use of number talks helps students solve all types of arithmetic problems with more accuracy, efficiency, and flexibility. And, while this number talk asked that students solve the problem mentally, others may require or allow students to use paper and pencils.

Number talks also present an alternative to traditional test-preparation activities. Write problems similar in content and format to those on standardized tests, and use number talks to demystify the various types of problems and strengthen students' understanding of those problems.

Ballpark Estimation

Overview

Through *Ballpark Estimation*, students relate estimation to items in their classroom. *Ballpark Estimation* is an easily adaptable activity that supports creative and divergent thinking. It also gives students an opportunity to apply benchmark numbers when estimating. Unlike an estimation jar activity, in which students focus on one particular container, *Ballpark Estimation* encourages students to consider many items and opens up multiple estimation opportunities in a single activity.

Activity Directions

1. Write a sentence frame on the board: *In our classroom there are about . . .*
2. Write a series of benchmark numbers below the sentence (e.g., *10, 25, 50, 75,* and *100*).
3. Ask students to think of ways to complete the sentence for each number. Let them discuss their ideas with their partners.
4. Write student responses on the board or an overhead transparency.

Key Questions

- How did you come up with your idea?
- Is there anything you already know that can help you make an estimate?
- Does anyone have a different way of thinking about it?

CONTENT AREA

Number and Operations

Measurement

MATERIALS

- optional: overhead projector

TIME

ten to fifteen minutes

From the Classroom

Lisa Kimbrell's third graders had a few minutes before an all-school assembly. I decided to introduce *Ballpark Estimation* to them. My meeting with the class was in mid-September, so they were just getting to know their teacher, the classroom routine, and each other. Presenting an activity that focused specifically on their classroom served dual purposes. It introduced them to mathematics in a relevant context while simultaneously helping familiarize them with their own classroom community.

I began the activity by writing on the whiteboard:

In our classroom there are about . . .

10	25	50	75	100

Then I began to explain the task. "This is an estimation activity. Would someone please remind us what it means to estimate?"

A few students raised their hands.

"It's when you make a guess," Angela responded.

"You think about some numbers," Scott added.

"It's like when you think about how many there are," Tony contributed.

"Yes," I agreed, "when you estimate you make a mathematical guess. You actually do math thinking and then use your ideas to estimate. When you make an estimate, are you supposed to know the exact answer?"

"No?" the class chorused somewhat uncertainly.

"Right," I said encouragingly. "You don't need to know the exact answer. If you knew the exact answer, you wouldn't need to estimate. So when you estimate, are you trying to get the exact right answer?"

"No." The class seemed a bit more confident this time.

"Does it matter whose estimate is closest to the exact number?"

"No."

"Do you win a new car if you're closest?"

"No."

"Does something terrible happen to you if your estimate is not the closest?"

"No!"

"OK," I confirmed. "Estimating is using your brain to think about numbers. The important part is your thinking, not being right or closest."

I really wanted to hammer this point home. If I could set a nonthreatening tone at the beginning of the year, it would pay off for a long time. Students need to feel that estimating is a risk-free and interesting endeavor. Teachers can encourage this perception by expressing interest in children's thought processes and de-emphasizing the actual total.

"So," I continued, "here's what I did. I wrote the beginning of a sentence on the board and below it I wrote some benchmark numbers."

I introduced the term *benchmark* in the course of the conversation, but I didn't want to get sidetracked with a long explanation or discussion. I knew that we would return to the idea of benchmarks throughout the year, so this was quick exposure to the idea. I wanted to keep the spotlight on estimation in this short period of time.

"Let's think about ten for a few moments. Can anyone think of something you have about ten of in this room?" I asked.

Many students looked around the room and quite a few began to count.

"Remember," I said, "you don't need to count to find exactly ten of something. You just need to find something that there are *about* ten of in the room."

I saw a few raised hands and called on Sandy.

"Those things," Sandy reported, pointing to some student-created graphs posted on construction paper.

"The surveys you made?" I asked. Math discussions often present occasions to help build vocabulary, especially with English learners.

"Yes," Sandy replied.

"How did you come up with that idea?" I asked.

Sandy explained, "It just sort of looks like ten."

I wrote *surveys* under the 10 on the board.

"The punctuation charts," William said, referring to a set of posters on the back wall.

I added his idea to the list.

"Now," I told the class, "I'm going to give you a minute to quietly talk to someone next to you about other things that might fit under the ten column. Remember, you don't need to count. You can look around the room, but don't leave your seats. Talk to each other and see what other ideas you can come up with."

From their brief partner talk, the students generated more items for the list. After they shared their ideas and I recorded them, I moved on to the bigger numbers. I had students partner up and discuss their ideas about items that would fit the rest of the benchmark numbers. Eavesdropping on the conversations offered a window into students' thinking and their number sense. Gladys pointed to a basket of markers and told her partner, Steven, that there were about twenty-five of them. Rico disagreed, estimating there were about seventy-five markers in the basket.

Some students continued to count items before offering any suggestions. This behavior told me that either the students had not had much prior experience with estimation or that they still were under the impression that it was important to be right or closest. In some cases, the items children shared were not estimates at all. For fifty, they suggested states on the map and stars on the flag. I chose to accept all ideas during this initial exposure to *Ballpark Estimation*. One of the nice things about these brief math activities is knowing that there will be a next time and that misconceptions can be addressed over time.

Several students had ideas that sparked a class discussion. Ruby estimated that there were about one hundred fingernails in the classroom. An issue arose as to whether toenails were part of the fingernail category. I helped establish that everyone had ten fingers and hence ten fingernails. Many students were still baffled by the prospect of estimating how many fingernails there were in the room and/or how to count them. Knowing that multiplication would be an important part of the math curriculum for that class, I decided to take a moment to focus on multiplicative thinking and how it might assist us in making estimates.

"How many fingernails does one person have?" I asked.

"Ten," the class responded in unison.

"How about two people?" I continued.

"Twenty."

"Four people?"

"Forty."

"What if we wanted to find out how many fingernails there were in the whole class?" I asked. "Can anyone think of a way to do that?"

"We could just count them," Sheila offered.

"How do you mean?" I probed.

"Like one, two, three," she explained.

"Yes," I agreed, "we could count by ones."

"Or we could count by tens," Kenny added.

"Or fives," Diana contributed.

"Great," I replied. "So if we're making estimates and it's a big number, there are some ways to think about it in small pieces. We can use numbers we know like ones, fives, and tens to help us estimate."

When we were adding to our lists, I challenged the class to come up with at least three things for each number. I stopped the students when the board looked like this:

In our classroom there are about . . .

10	25	50	75	100
Surveys	Math folders	Pattern blocks in a tub	Markers	Fingernails
Punctuation charts	Rectangles on the word wall	States on the map	Folders in the box	Books Papers
Names on the board	Board games	Stars on the flag	Dictionaries Ceiling tiles	Crayons in the crayon box
Books in the basket				
Blue tubs				
Posters				

I looked at our lists and began to wrap up. I wanted to plant the seed for a follow-up activity.

"I'm impressed with all of your ideas," I told the class. "You really seem to know what's in your classroom and you have some interesting ways to think about estimating. When I look at these lists, I see a lot of things that you could actually count to find out the exact totals. That might be an interesting activity to try sometime soon."

The students seemed intrigued by this notion. Although there wasn't time for them to compare actual totals with their estimates at that moment, I left the lists on the board, giving their teacher the opportunity to make these comparisons in the future. I thanked the students for their time and efforts and they headed off to their assembly.

Extending the Activity

I did this activity with young third graders. It is easily adaptable for the upper-elementary grades. Use different numbers with older students—fractions, decimals, percents, or larger numbers. *Ballpark Estimation* easily adjusts to whatever types of numbers the students are working with.

Another twist on the activity is to have students estimate about things beyond the classroom. The estimates can focus on an entire grade, the school, the neighborhood, or the city. This forces students to deal with larger numbers. They can collect data about their own class and use that information to make estimates about a larger group.

Ballpark Estimation can also become a measurement activity. Make a chart that says

> *Here are some things that are about . . .*
>
> *1 inch   6 inches   1 foot   2 feet   1 yard*

Teachers can also use this version of the activity to focus on two- or three-dimensional measurement. Ask students to consider items that measure in square or cubic units. Often students lack experience with measurement. This activity would give them repeated occasions to think about units of measurement, their relative size, and visual models that represent the approximate units.

Clear the Board

Overview

In this activity the class works together to generate the numbers one through twelve in order. The teacher begins the activity by rolling three dice. Using the results of the roll and any operations, the students create in consecutive order the numbers from one through twelve. Students may use the results of one die, two dice, or all three dice. When students encounter a number they cannot create using the results on the dice, the teacher rolls again. The activity is done when students have made all the numbers from one to twelve.

Clear the Board offers opportunities for mental computation and helps build number and operation sense. Students think flexibly and consider many possibilities in order to find solutions to the computation challenges involved.

Activity Directions

1. List vertically on the board or an overhead the numbers *1* through *12*.
2. Roll three dice and write the results of the roll on the board so everyone can see them.
3. Ask students if they see any ways to make the number one using the numbers rolled. One, two, or all three numbers rolled may be used in conjunction with any operation.
4. After students have created a way to make one, repeat Step 3 for the number two and record the solution on the board next to the 2.
5. Give students a few minutes to talk to each other about possible ways to make the next few numbers using the results of the first roll and any operation. Record their ideas on the board. When the next number is not possible, roll again. Record the results of the new roll on the board.
6. The activity is completed when the class has made every number on the board in order.

CONTENT AREA

Number and Operations

MATERIALS

- 3 dice
- optional: overhead projector

TIME

five to ten minutes

Key Questions

- How many rolls do you think it will take to clear the board?
- What numbers would you like to get now? Why?

From the Classroom

Amy Jackson wrote the numbers *1* through *12* vertically on the board before she said a word to her fourth and fifth graders. With their interest piqued, she asked them if they'd like to play a game. The response was quite positive.

"Great," she told the class. This game is called *Clear the Board*. Our goal is to systematically get rid of each number I listed. We have to get rid of the numbers in order, beginning with one first and then moving down to two, all the way to twelve.

"I'm going to roll three dice. I'll write the numbers rolled on the board so you can see them. Then you need to think about how you can use these numbers to make the number one. You may use any operation—addition, subtraction, multiplication, or division—or a combination of operations. When you find a way to make one, I'll clear the one off the board and we'll move on to the next number, two. Ready? Here I go."

Amy rolled a 1, a 3, and a 5. She wrote these numbers on the board.

Amy was surprised that students appeared to be struggling. Why didn't they just point out the 1? She wondered. Then she realized her directions might not have been clear enough.

"I need to clarify something," she told the class. "Even though there are three numbers, you don't need to use all of them. You can use one, two, or all three of the numbers rolled to make the number you need."

Marcello raised his hand. "How about five minus three minus one?" he suggested.

While Amy was expecting a simpler solution, she wrote Marcello's equation on the board next to the 1. Adriana suggested the need for parentheses around $5 - 3$. Technically parentheses are not required in this situation; however, their use is not incorrect and adds clarity. Amy decided to include them in the written model. She also pointed out that since they rolled a 1, they could use it as is. She wrote that on the board too.

$$1 \qquad (5 - 3) - 1 = 1, \quad 1 = 1$$

"OK, now that we've made one, we can cross it off. We're on our way to clearing the board. Next up is two."

"Three take away one is two," Enrique announced.

"You could also do five minus three," Jamal pointed out.

Amy wrote those two equations next to the 2 and then crossed off the 2. Once the students understood the mechanics of the activity, she gave them some time to talk in groups about ways to make the rest of the numbers. Soon the board filled up with a variety of solutions for the next few numbers. While Amy was impressed with the students' flexible thinking and comfort with mental computation, she was concerned that the game would go on and on if she didn't set a limit. The students were more interested in finding multiple solutions for each number than moving on to the next number. To keep the game moving, Amy decided to limit responses to one per number. In a few minutes the board looked like this:

~~1~~	$(5 - 3) - 1 = 1, 1 = 1$
~~2~~	$3 - 1 = 2, 5 - 3 = 2$
~~3~~	$3 = 3, (5 + 1) - 3 = 3, (5 - 3) + 1 = 3$
~~4~~	$3 + 1 = 4, 5 - 1 = 4$
~~5~~	$5 = 5, 5 \times 1 = 5, \frac{5}{1} = 5$
~~6~~	$5 + 1 = 6$
~~7~~	$(5 + 3) - 1 = 7$
~~8~~	$5 + 3 = 8$
~~9~~	$5 + 3 + 1 = 9$
~~10~~	$(3 - 1) \times 5 = 10$
11	
12	

The class was stuck on eleven, so Amy told the students it was time to roll again. Before rolling, she asked a question to stimulate more mental computation and to assess their comfort with the various operations.

"So," she said, "I'm going to roll the three dice again. What numbers would you like to get now?"

"A five, a six and a one," Cristina offered.

"A five, a six, and anything would work," Kendrick pointed out.

"How about a four, a four, and a three?" suggested Christine.

"Or a two, a three, and a six," J. P. added.

This quick question showed Amy that her students were comfortable breaking eleven apart in different ways but were not as comfortable thinking about operations other than addition. Perhaps with more time and practice they would open up their thinking.

She rolled the dice and got two 5s and a 1. She wrote these numbers on the board below where she'd written the first roll. Then she turned to the class.

"Tough one, huh?" she teased.

"Just put five plus one plus five," Kenyatta directed.

Amy wrote the equation next to the 11 on the board.

$5 + 1 + 5 = 11$

"Aren't you supposed to put parentheses, Ms. Jackson?" Jessie challenged.

"No," J. P. disagreed. "We don't need them."

"Let's check," Amy suggested.

She pointed to the first 5 and the 1.

"What's five plus one?" she asked the class.

"Six."

"Plus five more equals?"

"Eleven."

"OK," Amy continued, "let's see what happens if we start with the other two numbers."

She pointed to the 1 and the second 5.

"What's one plus five?" she asked.

"Six."

She pointed to the first 5.

"Plus five more?"

"Eleven."

"Hmm," she concluded, "we get the same answer regardless of where we start. So we don't really need parentheses for this addition equation."

She wrote on the board:

$(5 + 1) + 5 = 5 + (1 + 5)$

Although this wasn't the time to go into a lengthy discussion about the purpose of parentheses or the associative property, it was a nice opportunity to model the concept and notation briefly.

Amy gave the students a minute to talk to a partner about how to use these rolls to make twelve. After some computational gymnastics, the students agreed that they couldn't make twelve with those three numbers, so Amy rolled again. This time she got a 5, a 2, and a 1. She wrote these numbers on the board below the previous roll. The students took a minute to consider the possibilities. Christine raised her hand.

"I've got one," she announced. "Five plus one times two."

"Do I need to use parentheses for that equation?" Amy asked, reinforcing their prior discussion.

"Yes," Christine told her. "Put them around the five plus one."

Amy wrote the equation on the board and had the class double-check to make sure everyone agreed.

$(5 + 1) \times 2 = 12$

Amy crossed out the 12 on the board and congratulated the students for clearing the board. She asked how many rolls it took for them to accomplish their task. Since she had written each roll on the board, the students had an easy reference. Amy wondered aloud if they thought it would take more or less than three rolls when they played next time. Leaving them with something to think about set the stage for future experiences with *Clear the Board*.

Extending the Activity

There are many possible twists to this game. Introduce the activity as a whole-class, cooperative endeavor. Once students grasp the rules and goals, have them play a competitive version in pairs. Each student writes down the equations generated for each number in order to keep track of them all. In this version, partners can be challenged to use the same rolls to make their numbers. Students can compete to see who cleared the most numbers with a given roll. Or, each student can roll the dice for his or her turn and try to be the first to clear all twelve numbers.

The game can by extended by having students work their way from one through twelve and then back from twelve to one. Also, if students are relying too heavily on addition and subtraction, encourage or require the use of other operations as a challenge.

4

CONTENT AREA

Number and
Operations

MATERIALS

- 3-5 coins of
  different
  denominations
- clues about the
  coins, written on
  an index card
- a pocket, 0.35 mm
  film canister, or a
  small paper bag
- optional: overhead
  projector

TIME

ten to fifteen minutes

Coin Riddle

Overview

Riddles of all kinds intrigue children. Coin riddles stimulate children's logical thinking while simultaneously engaging them in arithmetic problems. In this activity students use clues and mental computation to systematically narrow down possibilities until they can identify the teacher's set of mystery coins.

To begin, hide a few coins in your pocket, in a 35 mm film canister, or in a small paper bag. Write clues to share with students to help them deduce the hidden coins. Give the students one clue at a time. Allow students to discuss all clues, make guesses about the identity of the coins, and check to make sure their guesses match the clues. Then reveal the coins. This activity can be adapted easily to the level and instructional focus of your class.

Activity Directions

1. Tell the students you have some coins in your pocket, a film canister, or a paper bag, and their job is to guess which coins.
2. With the help of students, make a list of possible coins you could have.
3. Give the clues one at a time, first recording a clue on the board or overhead and then reading it aloud. Encourage discussion after each new piece of information.
4. To model for students one way to organize information, draw a chart on the board and fill in the possible combinations of coins. (See page 21.)
5. Have students tell what coins they think you have.
6. Review each clue to make sure it fits the students' guess.
7. Reveal the coins.

Key Questions

- What do you know now about my secret coins?
- What can you eliminate?
- What are some possible coin combinations I might have?
- How do you know?

From the Classroom

I jingled the coins in my pocket as an introduction to the *Coin Riddle* activity.

"I have some coins in my pocket," I told Danielle Pickett's third graders.

"I can hear them!" Terrell noted enthusiastically.

"Are you going to use them for the bake sale?" Inca inquired.

"I didn't even know there was a bake sale today. Lucky me," I told her. "Maybe I will use them for the bake sale later, but for now I'm going to use them for a math activity."

Before introducing the actual riddle, I decided to tap into the students' prior knowledge and get them thinking about coins in general.

"So, does anyone have any ideas about what coins might be in my pocket?" I asked the class.

"Maybe pennies," Jaime volunteered.

"I think it's quarters," Tracie offered.

"It could be pesos," Josue posited, eliciting giggles from other students.

"Well, I do love to go to Mexico," I told the class, "but today I've only got U.S. coins. So if you know that the coins are American, what are the possible coins I could have in my pocket? Talk to a partner about what you know about coins and what my secret coins might be."

After a minute or so I asked for the class's attention and had volunteers tell me a coin. As the students told me a coin, I asked for its value. I wrote the names and values on the board so students would have a reference. Several of the third graders in Danielle's class were English learners so I wanted to be sure they weren't constrained by vocabulary.

penny = 1 cent

nickel = 5 cents

dime = 10 cents

quarter = 25 cents

half-dollar = 50 cents

dollar = 100 cents

I jingled the coins again to refocus the students. "There are a lot of different coins. I'm going to help you by narrowing the possibilities down a bit. I'll tell you that for this activity the coins could be pennies, nickels, dimes, or quarters."

I put a box around those four coins on the board to remind students where to focus.

"So here's what happens next," I announced as I pulled an index card out of a different pocket. "I have a riddle about my mystery coins. The riddle will give you clues to help you figure out what coins I have in my pocket. As I share the clues, you'll be able to talk to a partner about what you know about my coins and what you think they might be. There also might be some clues that tell you what my coins aren't. That information could help you eliminate some of the possibilities. Are you ready?"

"Yes!" the children responded.

"OK," I said, "here's my first clue. After I write it on the board, you need to think about how this clue helps you think about what coins I might have." I wrote on the board:

I have three coins.

We read this clue aloud together. Then I had students turn to a partner and brainstorm what the three coins might be. I let five or six students volunteer their ideas and we agreed that there were a lot of possibilities. Then I wrote another clue on the board:

They are all different.

"How does that clue help you?" I asked the class.

Nikki responded, "We know it's not three pennies or three quarters or anything like that."

"Also, it can't be, like, two dimes and a nickel because they're all different," Kendra added.

"Hmm," I said. "I wonder if we could figure out what coin combinations would fit my clues. Maybe a chart to show all the possible combinations would help."

I drew a chart on the board. While not integral to the *Coin Riddle* activity, the chart provided another visual reference for students and also offered a model of how to systematically organize information. The class and I filled in the chart together.

Pennies	Nickels	Dimes	Quarters	Total Value
1	1	1		
1		1	1	
1	1		1	
	1	1	1	

"It looks like we've got it narrowed down to four possibilities. Now let's see if the next clue can help you narrow it down even further," I told the class as I wrote the next clue on the board:

Their total value is more than 20 cents and less than 50 cents.

I gave the students a few minutes to talk about this new information and how it could help them. During their discussion they did a lot of mental computation to determine the value of each combination on the chart.

"Can we eliminate anything?" I asked the class.

"It's not one penny, one nickel, and one dime," Chastity announced.

"How do you know?" I probed.

"Because that only adds up to sixteen cents," Alex explained. "Because ten plus five is fifteen plus one more makes sixteen."

"Oh, I see," I told him. "So we can cross this off the chart."

I crossed off the penny-nickel-dime option. I also took a moment to have the class tell me the total value of the other coin combinations. I wrote the values in the last column of the chart on the board. Then I wrote the next clue:

Two of the coins are silver and one is copper.

I saw immediately that some of the students were confused by this clue. In particular, the English learners looked quizzical.

"What does this mean?" I asked the class. "What is silver? What is copper?"

"Your watch is silver," Ignacio pointed out.

"Yes," I agreed, pointing to my watch, "this is silver. It's a kind of color for metal. What else do you see that is silver?"

"Ms. Pickett's ring."

"The doorknob."

"The shelf under the whiteboard."

After it was clear the students knew what *silver* meant, I asked them which coins were silver. They easily identified the nickel, the dime, and the quarter. I told them that the penny was copper. We briefly talked about other copper things to be sure they understood.

"So now what do you know about the secret coins?" I queried.

"One of the coins is a penny and the others are nickels, dimes, or quarters," Sally shared.

"All right, here's the last clue," I told the class as I wrote on the board:

I have no nickels.

"Talk to a partner about how this helps you figure out what coins I have in my pocket. You might also want to use the chart we made to help you," I suggested.

Soon, the students knew which coins I had. In unison on the count of three, I had them tell me what mystery coins I had. I referred back to the chart and to the clues on the board to confirm with them that their solution fit all the criteria. Finally, I pulled the coins out of my pocket to show the class.

"You're right," I told them. "I had a penny, a dime, and a quarter in my pocket." After the cheers subsided, I congratulated the students on their excellent logical thinking. I encouraged them to try to make up their own coin riddle challenges for the next time I visited.

Extending the Activity

Because I was introducing *Coin Riddle* for the first time, I used a whole-class, teacher-directed approach. As students become familiar with the activity, they can take on more ownership. For example, I could reveal the clues all at once and let partners or groups discuss the possibilities and try to solve the riddle.

Students can also write their own coin riddles that can be collected and used for future *Coin Riddle* sessions. Before sending students off to write their own riddles, make sure they understand what makes an effective clue. The clue must reveal some helpful information but not completely give the answer away. For example, "The total value is my lucky number" is not a helpful clue. And a clue such as "I have four coins and they equal four cents" gives too much away. The students need to understand that the group of clues taken together leads to the one correct solution. It's a good idea to start by leading the whole class in writing a riddle together. Predetermining the coins can help as well. While it may take a while for students to create viable riddles on their own, it's worth the investment. Students develop their logical thinking and language through both generating and solving coin riddles.

The riddle activity transfers nicely to a geometry context. Begin by modeling a riddle about a shape. It could be two-dimensional or three-dimensional, depending on students' familiarity with various shapes and geometry vocabulary. Have students discuss and solve your riddle. When students are ready, assign a shape to a pair or group of students. Have them work on writing a riddle about their assigned shape. Writing and solving shape riddles helps students develop their geometry vocabulary and concepts.

5

Comparing Fractions

CONTENT AREA

Number and
Operations

MATERIALS

- a die or spinner
  numbered 1–6
- optional: projector

TIME

five to fifteen minutes

Overview

The study of fractions is often a great challenge for upper-elementary students. Many students get bogged down in notation and computational procedures. In order to combat this tendency, we need to give students ongoing opportunities to make sense of fractions. *Comparing Fractions* affords students a chance to connect fraction symbols with visual images and to explore both the relationship between numerators and denominators and the relative size of different fractions.

Activity Directions

1. Have each student draw a game board on a piece of paper.

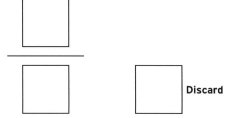

2. Roll the die or spin the spinner and let students decide whether they want to use the number as the numerator, use it as the denominator, or discard it.
3. Roll two more times, each time allowing the students to place the resulting number in the box of their choice. If a resulting roll is a repeat number, roll again in order to have three different numbers.
4. Have each student draw a picture of the fraction he or she created.
5. Ask students to tell you what fractions they made. Record the fractions and pictures on the board or an overhead transparency.

6. Lead a class discussion about the relative size of the fractions and how the students know which is bigger or smaller. During the discussion, place the fractions in the appropriate locations on a number line.

7. Play again as a class and try to make as small a fraction as possible.

Key Questions

- Which is the smallest fraction? Which is the largest? How do you know?
- Where does this fraction fit on the number line?
- What number would you like to get? Why?

From the Classroom

I introduced *Comparing Fractions* with a very open-ended, nonthreatening approach. Knowing that many students are shaky when it comes to fractions, I wanted to make sure everyone felt comfortable and competent. I didn't want anyone to shut down because of a lack of confidence in his or her understanding of fractions. Once I got the students engaged, I planned to ramp up the difficulty level.

"I've got a new activity for you," I told a group of fourth and fifth graders. "It's called *Comparing Fractions*. I have a die that I will roll. The results of the rolls will determine the fraction you make. It will probably make more sense once we get started. Let's do one round together. To begin you need to draw a recording sheet that looks like this." I drew a sample recording sheet on the board.

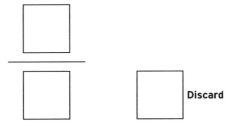

I rolled a 3. I explained to the class, "Now you each need to decide if you want to use the results of the roll as the numerator, the denominator, or a discard. The discard box is like a trash can. You're throwing that number away and it's not going to be part of your fraction. Once you put a number in a box, you can't change it. So go ahead and write a *three* in whichever box you want."

I rolled twice more, resulting in a 4 and a 1. After each roll I told the students the results of the roll and gave them a few moments to write the number in the box of their choosing. After the students had created their fractions, I asked them to each draw a sketch of what their fraction looked like. In this way the students connected the symbols to a visual representation. I then asked volunteers to tell what fraction they made and describe their picture of it. Some of the students had made improper fractions, so we had a brief discussion about what mathematicians call these fractions and how to draw them. I recorded all the fractions and their pictures on the board:

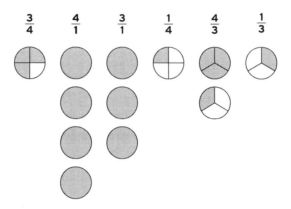

"So you were able to make six different fractions," I noted. "Let's compare these fractions and think about where they would fit on a number line."

I drew a long number line on the board and labeled it with a *0* on the left end and a *1* about one-fourth of the way across.

"Talk to a partner," I told the students. "Discuss where these fractions belong on the number line. You can use the numbers and the pictures to help you think about which is the biggest and smallest and where the others fit in between."

The students seemed confused, so I decided to break down the task and model a bit of it with them. "What is the smallest fraction up here?" I asked, pointing to the board.

"One-fourth," Kalen offered.

"How do you know?" I asked.

"Because look at the pictures," Kalen responded. "You can see it's the smallest."

"Also fourths are smaller than thirds or ones," Brittany added. "And if you only have one fourth, you're going to have the least."

"OK," I agreed. "So where would one-fourth go on this number line?"

"It goes after the zero but before the one because it's less than one," Veronika shared.

"Does it go right in the middle between zero and one?" I pressed.

"No," Michael replied. "That's where one-half would go. One-fourth is one-half of a half, so it goes closer to zero."

I approximated the location for one-fourth and labeled it on the number line.

"The smallest fraction you made is now on the number line," I continued. "Let's put the largest fraction up here too. Which fraction is the largest?"

"Four ones," Chad responded.

"Yes," I agreed, "I'm looking at all the pictures on the board, and four is definitely the largest number. Where do we put it?"

"It goes way past the one," Claire announced. "Like on a regular number line it goes one, two, three, four."

"This isn't a regular number line?" I asked.

"Not really," Claire explained, "because we're putting fractions on it."

"You can put fractions on a number line," Jessica disagreed.

I took the opportunity to clarify some possible misconceptions about fractions and number lines.

"This is an interesting discussion," I told the class. "A lot of times when we think about numbers, we think of whole numbers or counting numbers. There are actually other types of numbers too."

"Like negative numbers," Cole volunteered.

"Right," I agreed. "Fractions and decimals are numbers too. A number line is a tool we use to help us think about numbers. Number lines are helpful when we want to compare numbers. They also can be helpful for addition or subtraction. Right now we're using a number line to compare fractions and put them in order from smallest to largest."

"Claire told us that four is the largest fraction and it goes to the right of the one," I continued. "I'm going to put it on the number line. Then you're going to have a few minutes to talk with a partner about where the other fractions fit on our number line. You can also use your papers to draw a number line and place the fractions where you think they belong."

I wrote *4* on the number line and gave the students some time to talk to each other. They had many tools available—the number line, the pictures of the fractions, their own paper to sketch on, and each other to talk to. Providing multiple access avenues is extremely important when students are grappling with new or challenging mathematical ideas. I called the class back to attention and we placed the rest of the fractions on the number line. Then I moved the students on to a more challenging task.

"This time, let's try to make a small fraction, as close to zero as possible." I rolled a 2 and asked the students which box to put it in.

"Don't put it as the denominator," warned Demetrius.

"Why not?" I asked.

"Because then it will be a half. That's already far away from zero," Demetrius explained.

"So where do you recommend we put the two?" I asked.

"I say throw it in the trash," he suggested.

I wrote *2* in the discard box and rolled the die again. This time the result was a *5*.

"Where do you want to put it?" I asked the class.

"Put it on the bottom," Sheila directed.

"Why do you want a five as the denominator?" I queried while using proper terminology.

"The only number higher is six, and you probably won't get a six. You want a big number for the denominator because that means you sliced it into more little pieces."

"OK," I continued as I wrote *5* in the denominator box. "So we've got one more roll. Take a few moments to talk to a partner about what roll you're hoping for. What number would you like as the numerator to get a fraction close to zero? Talk about why you're hoping for that number."

I gave the students some time to consider the possibilities. Many of them drew pictures to help them. There was consensus that a 1 would be the best possible number to use as the numerator. I rolled the die and the result was a 3.

"Oh man!" Jerome lamented. "That's way too big."

"Well," I responded, "it doesn't seem that bad to me. You had a two, a three, and a five to work with. What fraction could you have made that would have been smaller than three-fifths?"

"We could have made two-fifths," Samantha noted.

"Yes," I replied as I gestured toward the number line, "you could have gotten a little closer to zero with two-fifths. Are there any other fractions you could have made that are closer to zero?"

"That's the smallest fraction we could make," Tony stated.

"How do you know?" I challenged.

"Because five was the biggest number and we made it the denominator, so that means we had the most little pieces possible. Then if we put two as the numerator, it would be the least number of those little pieces."

I restated Tony's conjecture. "So you're saying that if you want a small fraction, you need a big denominator and a little numerator. Let's think about that for a moment. Look at the fractions we have on the board, talk to a partner, and see what you think about Tony's idea."

I gave the students a bit of time to discuss the relationship between the numerator and the denominator. Again, the pictures proved very useful in clarifying the concepts and connecting the symbols to quantities. I left the students with another question to ponder.

"So," I summarized, "it seems like you're starting to develop a theory about how to make the smallest fraction possible with three rolls of the die. The next time I visit, we'll try to make the largest fraction with three rolls. I wonder if you can come up with some ideas about how to do that."

Extending the Activity

Partners can play *Comparing Fractions*, working either cooperatively or competitively to make the smallest or largest fraction possible.

Comparing Fractions can easily be adjusted to the particular fraction concept being studied. If students are working on computation, have them make a game board that requires them to add, subtract, multiply, or divide. For example, you might challenge them to make the largest product using a game board like this:

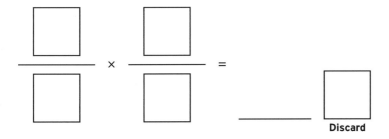

In addition, all versions of the activity can be used with decimals rather than fractions. Regardless of the version of the activity, students must have access to visual tools to help them make sense of the numbers they make and the computation they do. Have them draw pictures and/or use a number line.

6

Coordinate Tic-Tac-Toe

CONTENT AREA

Algebra

MATERIALS

- *Coordinate Tic-Tac-Toe* grids, several for each pair of students (see Blackline Masters)
- optional: overhead projector

TIME

five to fifteen minutes

Overview

In *Coordinate Tic-Tac-Toe*, students practice using ordered pairs and coordinate graphs in a game context. The game uses the strategy and mechanics of tic-tac-toe with a few twists. Partners try to get four points in a row horizontally, vertically, or diagonally on the coordinate graph. Also, Xs and Os are marked on the intersections of lines rather than in spaces.

Activity Directions

1. Make a coordinate graph on the board or an overhead transparency. Discuss with students how to use a coordinate graph.

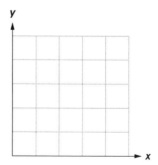

2. Draw a T-chart on the board and label the columns *Teacher: X* and *Class: O*.

Teacher: X	Class: O

3. Begin the game by recording an ordered pair on the T-chart, plotting the corresponding point on the grid, and marking it with an X (e.g., (4, 2)).

4. Have a student choose an ordered pair. Record it on the Class side of the T-chart and mark the corresponding point on the graph with an O.

5. Continue taking turns until one side has a line of four points in a row.

6. Let students play additional games with partners.

Key Questions

- Why did you pick that point?
- What strategy did you use?

From the Classroom

"I've got a game for you today," I announced to Tina Rasori's class of fourth graders. "It might seem familiar in some ways. It's called *Coordinate Tic-Tac-Toe*."

I drew a 5-by-5 coordinate graph on the board. I knew the students had been working on graphing activities lately, so I did a very quick review. "Do you know what this type of graph is called?" I asked.

I was met with blank stares.

"It's called a *coordinate graph*," I told the class. "These graphs are very useful in algebra. They can show how patterns grow and shrink. They can also show how something moves or changes over time. Today we're going to play a game that will help you understand how to plot points on a coordinate graph. Ordered pairs are used to name points on the graph. For example, if I wrote the ordered pair (three, four), where do you think I'd plot, or mark, my point?"

I wrote on the board:

(3, 4)

"Go over three and up four," Jose instructed.

"Where do I start?" I asked.

"Where the axes cross," Cindy explained.

"OK," I said as I modeled on the board, "starting at the origin where the axes cross at zero, I go over three on the *x*-axis and up four. The point for this ordered pair is (three, four)." As I talked with the students, I put my finger on the origin and moved it to the right along the *x*-axis, counting aloud, "One, two, three." When I reached the 3, I counted up four, moving my finger and counting aloud as I did so.

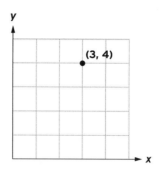

I deliberately modeled the physical plotting of the point along with incorporating the proper vocabulary so that students would become comfortable and familiar with the terminology and structure.

Next I explained the rules for the games. "In *Coordinate Tic-Tac-Toe*, you need to get four in a row instead of three in a row, and Xs and Os go on the intersections of lines rather than in spaces, like regular tic-tac-toe. I'll be Xs and the class can be Os. I'll start by putting an X on (three, two)."

I drew a T-chart and a new graph on the board. I recorded my ordered pair on the left side of the T-chart and then starting at the origin, I modeled, as before, how to plot my ordered pair on the grid.

Teacher: X	Class: O
(3, 2)	

"Now it's your turn. You need to think about where you want your O and what ordered pair describes that point," I told the class.

"How about (four, three)?" Martin suggested.

I added Martin's ordered pair to the right side of the T-chart and carefully plotted the point, beginning at the origin, counting aloud to four as I moved my finger along the *x*-axis, counting aloud to three, as I moved up the *y*-axis, and marking the O on the graph in the appropriate place.

"Hmm," I pondered as I looked at the graph, "I think I'll take (three, one)."

I recorded my ordered pair on the left side of the T-chart and then again plotted it on the graph by beginning at the origin and counting aloud as I moved my finger along the *x*-axis to 3 and then up one. Then I called on Sofi to take a turn for the class.

"Definitely (three, three)," she stated.

"Why did you pick that point?" I asked her.

"Because I want to try to block you," she explained.

"Aha," I responded, "that's interesting. There are really a couple of things going on in this game. You want to get four in a row, but you also have to pay attention to what your partner is doing. You might find you develop some strategies as you play this game."

I added Sofi's data to the board, carefully continuing to model how to plot points.

Teacher: X	Class: O
(3, 2)	(4, 3)
(3, 1)	(3, 3)

The game continued until the class had gotten four Os in a row. I deliberately let the students win this introductory game both to build their confidence and to model being a good sport. Next I gave each pair of students a *Coordinate Tic-Tac-Toe* grid (see Blackline Masters) and gave them a few minutes to play the game on their own. The students enjoyed the game immensely and I encouraged them to teach it to someone at home. I knew that as students played *Coordinate Tic-Tac-Toe* throughout the year, they would continue to develop strategies and build a solid foundation with coordinate graphing.

Extending the Activity

There are many ways to extend this activity. You can let students make their own coordinate grids for practice with constructing the graphs, but I usually start by providing prepared *Coordinate Tic-Tac-Toe* grids, because sometimes when students draw their own coordinate graphs freehand, the graphs are sloppy or slanted, making it difficult for students to see if they have four in a row.

Another way to extend the activity is to have a strategy talk with the class. Have students share what they have noticed after playing several times with their partners. Discuss strategies they used and why they seem to work. After students have had whole-class discussions about their strategies, they can do some writing about them. Ask students to each describe a strategy they use and explain why it works.

Also, as students become adept at the activity, they can try a challenge. Have them use a four-quadrant coordinate graph that includes negative numbers.

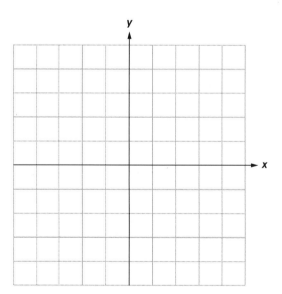

This version of the activity gives children exposure to negative numbers in a game context. It also prepares them for using these graphs in future algebra activities.

Digit Place

7

Overview

Students use a great deal of logic and language in this guessing game. As they make guesses and receive clues, they zero in on the secret number. Guidance from the teacher helps students see the progression of their guesses and how to make conjectures that narrow down the possibilities and lead to finding the mystery number.

To begin, choose a three-digit number with no two digits the same. Invite the class to guess your number. After each guess, tell the class how many digits in the guess are correct and how many of the correct digits are in the correct place.

Activity Directions

1. Think of a secret three-digit number with no repeating digits (e.g., 332 has two 3s in it, so it's not a good secret number for this game).
2. Make a recording chart on the board or an overhead with three columns, labeled *Guess, Digit,* and *Place.*

Guess	Digit	Place

3. Have a student guess a three-digit number (with no repeating digits) and record it in the Guess column.
4. In the Digit column, write the number of digits that match your secret number.
5. In the Place column, write the number of correct digits that are in the correct place in your secret number.

CONTENT AREA

Number and Operations

MATERIALS

- optional: overhead projector

TIME

ten to fifteen minutes

6. Have another student use the information from the previous guess to guess a new three-digit number. Record as described in Steps 3–5.
7. Stop periodically to have students discuss what they know about the number and what number they'd like to guess next.
8. Continue until the class is able to guess your secret number.

Key Questions

- What do you know about my secret number?
- What next guess would you like to make? Why?
- How does this clue help you?
- What digits can you eliminate? Explain.

From the Classroom

"You might have played this game before," I told Robin Gordon's fourth graders. "But it is such a fun one that you can play it over and over. It's called *Digit Place*. Has anyone played it before?"

Several students said they knew the game, while others smiled uncertainly. I could tell this would be an introduction for many of the students, so I knew I'd need to model carefully and check in with the students frequently.

"Here's how it works," I explained. "I'm going to think of a three-digit number and you're going to try to guess it." (Prior to starting the game I decided my secret number would be 619.) "I'll give you clues each time you guess and the clues should help you narrow down the possibilities and figure out my secret number. So what is the lowest three-digit number?"

"One hundred," Raquel blurted out.

"OK," I said, "and what's the highest three-digit number?"

"Nine hundred ninety-nine," William responded.

I wrote on the board:

100–999

"So my three-digit number is somewhere between one hundred and nine hundred ninety-nine," I told the class. "However, it can't be one hundred or nine hundred ninety-nine because when you play this game you need to choose a number that doesn't have any repeating digits. One hundred has two zeros and nine hundred ninety-nine has three nines. The number I picked has three different digits. So, you know my number is somewhere between one hundred and nine hundred ninety-nine and you know it has three different digits. Who would like to make a guess?"

Many hands shot into the air. I called on Alexa, who guessed 413. I drew a recording chart with three columns on the board and recorded her number in the Guess column. Then I wrote a *1* in the Digit column and a *1* in the Place column.

Guess	Digit	Place
413	1	1

"You guessed four hundred thirteen. You have one digit and one place correct. What does that mean?" I asked the class.

"It means that your secret number has a four or a one or a three in it," Ricky explained.

"And it's in the right place," Ishmael added.

I asked for a volunteer to make another guess.

"How about five hundred thirty-seven?" Miguel suggested.

I added his guess to the board with the corresponding clues.

Guess	Digit	Place
413	1	1
537	0	0

"Sometimes kids think a guess with no correct digits and places is a bad guess," I told the class, "but actually it's very helpful. How does this help you think about my secret number?"

Betty explained, "Zero digits tells you not to guess those numbers."

"Yeah," Victor added, "you know there's not a five or three or seven in your number."

I wrote the digits *0* through *9* on the board and crossed out the 3, the 5, and the 7.

0   1   2   3̸   4   5̸   6   7̸   8   9

"Miguel's guess helps you eliminate some digits and focus your guesses on the remaining possibilities," I summarized. Writing the digits on the board and crossing them out along the way can help students focus and organize their thinking. It also encourages the kind of deductive reasoning that is essential in this game.

I took several more guesses. From these guesses, the students were able to eliminate two more digits, which I crossed off the list on the board. Then I had the students talk to a partner about what they thought they knew about my number, what next guess they'd like to make, and why that guess would be helpful.

$$\cancel{0} \quad 1 \quad \cancel{2} \quad 3 \quad \cancel{4} \quad \cancel{5} \quad 6 \quad \cancel{7} \quad 8 \quad 9$$

Guess	Digit	Place
413	1	1
537	0	0
124	1	0
125	1	0
410	1	1
403	0	0

I called for the class's attention and shifted the discussion to the logical thinking.

"A lot of you are raising your hands right now," I observed, "and I'm assuming that means you'd like to make a guess. That's great, but if you want to make a guess, you also need to explain why you're picking that number and how you think it will help."

I paused for a moment to let that sink in. Then I called on Ontario.

"We want to guess eight hundred nineteen because we know there can only be a one, six, eight, or nine in your number. Also we think the one goes in the tens place."

"Why do you think that?" I prompted.

"Because when you look at one hundred twenty-four and one hundred twenty-five, they both have one digit correct but it's in the wrong place. Then on four hundred ten, there's one digit correct and it's in the right place. And we know it has to be the one because we already crossed off the other digits."

"Does that make sense?" I asked the class.

Many students nodded because they had made similar discoveries in their small-group discussions. I knew some students might not follow Ontario's logic, but they would still benefit from being reminded that math is about making sense. I added *819* to the chart and told the students that they had two digits correct and two places correct. There was a great deal of excitement and many hands were eagerly waving. I decided to slow it down and have the students talk again before making more guesses.

"OK," I acknowledged, "you've got a lot of ideas about my number at this point. Here's what you need to do. Talk to your partner again. This time discuss what you know about my secret number and what guess would give you the most information and help you figure out what the secret number is. Make sure you can explain why this guess will be so helpful."

I gave the students about a minute to talk to each other. Then I called on Cynthia.

"We want to guess six hundred nineteen," she announced. "We know the one is correct and we know either the eight or the nine is correct. So we're going to test out the six and see whether the eight or the nine is in the right place."

"How will you know?" I asked.

"Because if you say we only have one digit and one place correct, we'll know we need to put the eight back."

"And if you say three digits correct, we'll know we got your number," Tanner added.

I wrote *619* on the chart and put a *3* in the Digit column and a *3* in the Place column. The students cheered. They had found my number.

"Wow," I observed, looking at the game chart, "my number could have been almost any number between one hundred and nine hundred ninety-nine. It took you only eight guesses to get it. That's the power of logical thinking."

I congratulated the students on a game well played and encouraged them to continue trying their skills at *Digit Place* in the future.

Extending the Activity

Often, I'll introduce *Digit Place* using a two-digit number. That way students become familiar with the rules and terminology before they have to use a great deal of logical thinking. Since a significant number of Robin's students already knew the game, I decided to jump right into a three-digit version. When in doubt, opt for the easier game to ensure success and a positive attitude about the upcoming challenge.

Once students are quite familiar with *Digit Place*, they can play on their own with partners. Even better than one-on-one games are games where pairs play against each other. This gives students someone to check their ideas and also prompts more communication throughout the game. Students can choose a two-, three-, or even four-digit number to guess.

Also, if students are curious about why the secret numbers need to have three different digits, they might want to investigate. Allow them to try using a number with repeating digits to see what happens and how clues become confusing.

Digit Place also offers an excellent writing opportunity. After students have played multiple games, they can write about strategies they use and how they determine which numbers to guess.

Dot Clusters

8

Overview

The connections between numbers and geometry are often overlooked in the traditional math curriculum. Visual and spatial learners benefit from ways to see physical models of numbers rather than just think of them as quantities or symbols. *Dot Clusters* provides a concrete, geometric way for students to see numbers as groups of objects and think about computation in a visual way. *Dot Clusters* also gives students practice connecting a visual model to its symbolic equation.

Activity Directions

1. Scatter ten beans on the overhead before turning it on. You might want to start with a random scattering or you might choose to make a deliberate configuration.
2. Tell students they need to figure out how many beans are on the overhead without counting by ones.
3. Turn on the overhead and let students find the total number of beans.
4. Discuss the different ways students grouped the beans to find the answer.
5. Repeat the activity with twelve beans.
6. Show students the *Dot Clusters* overhead (see Blackline Masters). Let them look at it for a few moments and discuss with their partners how they might group the dots.

CONTENT AREA

Number and Operations

Geometry

MATERIALS

- overhead projector
- 12 beans
- *Dot Clusters* overhead transparency (see Blackline Masters)
- *Dot Clusters* recording sheets, 1 per student (see Blackline Masters)
- overhead transparency of *Dot Clusters* recording sheet

TIME

five to fifteen minutes

7. Pass out the *Dot Clusters* recording sheets (see Blackline Masters).

8. Tell students they need to use equal groupings to find different ways to total the dot clusters on their sheets. Have students record the corresponding equation for each dot grouping.

9. Share and discuss the students' grouping strategies and equations.

Key Questions

- Where did you start?
- What did you see?
- Can you write an equation that describes how you did it?

From the Classroom

I greeted Amy Jackson's fourth and fifth graders by telling them I had brought a bag of pinto beans with me. After clarifying what a pinto bean was and showing them a sample, I moved on to the math activity.

"So I have some pinto beans," I explained to the class. "I'm going to put them on the overhead. Your job is to try to figure out how many pinto beans are on the overhead. The challenge is to try not to count by ones. See if there are ways you can group the beans to make it easier to count."

"When we count, can it be an estimate?" Kesha asked.

"That's a great question," I responded. "A lot of times an estimate is good enough. In this activity, however, you need to figure out exactly how many beans there are. You might want to do a quick estimate first, but your answer should be the actual number of beans on the overhead."

I had ten beans in my hand. I put them on the overhead in several clusters.

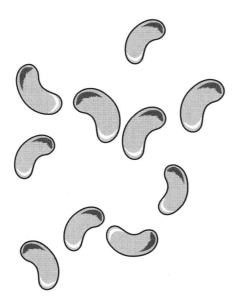

Then I turned on the overhead and gave the students a minute or so to see the beans and find the total. I asked for the students' attention so we could discuss what they saw and did.

"Nod your head if you know how many beans are up here," I said to the class.

There were nods all around. I had the whole group say the total in unison so we could get right to the interesting part of the activity. I asked students to share what they saw and how they had grouped the beans to find the total. There were a variety of responses as the children shared their thinking.

"I counted by twos," David explained.

"I counted by threes," Brandy shared.

Adriana told us she saw three groups of three plus one more. Kesha saw four, four, and two. As each child shared, I tried to clarify and connect his or her ideas to the bean configuration on the overhead. I pointed to the clusters of beans and asked questions that helped connect the numbers to the visual model, such as "Where did you start?" and "Is this what you saw?"

I repeated the activity again, this time using twelve beans. I encouraged the students to look for equal groups that could make counting and finding the total easier. Finding equal groups facilitates the use of multiplication, which is more efficient. After we had discussed ways they saw the twelve beans, we moved on.

"So now I have a challenge for you," I announced to the class. "You've had a little practice looking at beans and grouping them in ways that help you find the total. This time I've got a sheet with a bunch of dots. You need to find ways to group these dots to help you figure out how many there are. I'll give you a minute or two to talk to a partner about how you might group these dots. Then you'll get a chance to go back to your tables and work on your own sheet of dots."

I put the *Dot Clusters* transparency on the overhead for the children to see. They talked and pointed at the model and I knew they were ready to begin working.

"OK," I told them, "you've got some ideas about how to approach this problem. I have a sheet for each of you. There are six pictures of this group of dots on it. Your challenge is to see if you can find six different ways to group the dots using equal groupings and find the total. The extra challenge is for you to write an equation that describes each way you grouped the dots."

"Can we work with a partner?" William queried.

"I think it's a great idea to work together on this. When you go back to your tables, you'll each have your own recording sheet, but you can talk together and share your grouping strategies with each other."

I passed out the recording sheets and the children got to work. As I circulated around the tables, I noticed that some students were simply circling groups of two or three dots and not necessarily looking at the bigger picture. I decided to interrupt them briefly.

"I'm noticing that you're doing a good job of using equal groups," I told them. "Make sure you're looking at the whole cluster before you make those groups, though. There might be some ways you can chunk bigger groups of dots together. Think about the symmetry of the design. That might help you see groups in different ways."

The students got back to work and I walked around with an overhead transparency of the *Dot Clusters* recording sheet and pen. I copied a variety of students' arrangements onto the overhead. Then I called the students back to the rug and put the overhead up for them to see.

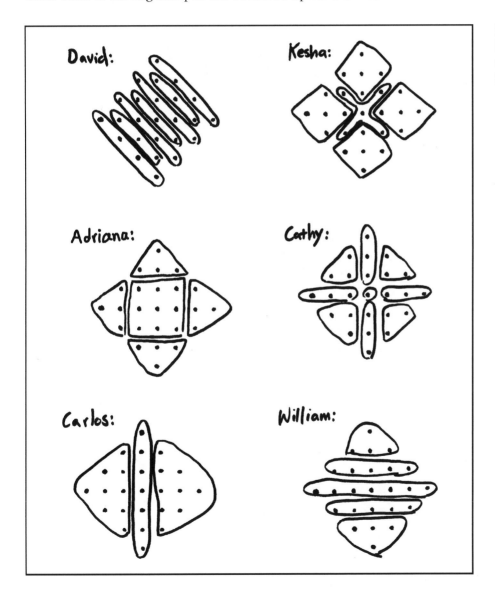

Figure 8-1 An overhead showing different ways students grouped the dots.

"You found a lot of ways to solve this problem," I complimented. "I picked a few to share with the class. As you look at them, see if you can figure out what each person did. Also, think about equations that could describe the different groupings. I'll let you talk to a partner for a minute about that."

I gave the students a minute to look at the samples on the overhead and talk about equations.

"So let's start with Cathy's," I suggested. "Can anyone describe what Cathy did?"

"She grouped them by threes," Blake noted.

"And there was one left over in the middle," Kesha added.

"How many groups of three did she find?" I asked.

"Eight," several students responded at once.

"Hmm," I said, "so how can we write an equation to explain Cathy's way?"

"It's eight times three plus one more," Ruby answered.

"How do I write that?" I asked.

"Put parentheses around eight times three and then write plus one," Isaac explained.

Next to Cathy's work on the overhead I wrote:

$$(8 \times 3) + 1 = 25$$

"Does that look right?" I asked the class.

There were nods of approval. We moved on to add equations to the rest of the examples on the overhead. When we were done, the overhead looked like Figure 8–2 (see page 47).

I told the children I was impressed with their ability to connect pictures to equations. I encouraged them to continue trying to picture what equations might look like.

Extending the Activity

Dot clusters and bean clusters are highly adaptable. Do this as a quickie activity and just put some beans on the overhead when there are a spare few minutes of class time. Giving students recording sheets extends the activity and allows opportunities for discussions about equations. Create *Dot Clusters* sheets with different amounts of dots and different configurations. In any incarnation, the activity encourages students to use geometric models to solve numeric problems.

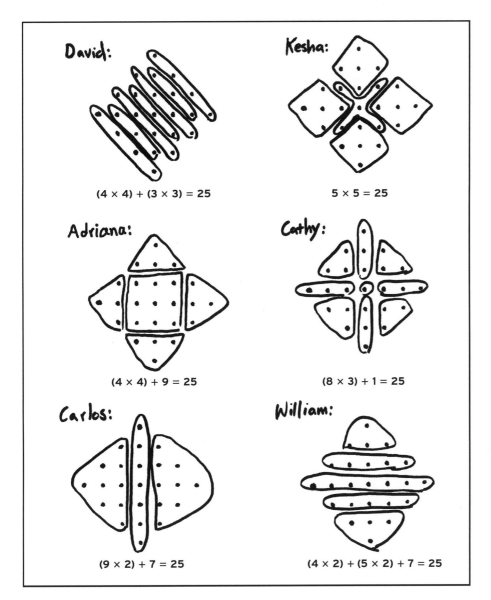

David:

(4 × 4) + (3 × 3) = 25

Kesha:

5 × 5 = 25

Adriana:

(4 × 4) + 9 = 25

Cathy:

(8 × 3) + 1 = 25

Carlos:

(9 × 2) + 7 = 25

William:

(4 × 2) + (5 × 2) + 7 = 25

Figure 8-2 Equations explain how students grouped the dots.

A literature connection can be made with books such as Greg Tang's *The Grapes of Math* (New York: Scholastic, 2001). You can read this book aloud to offer students visual situations in which they will be encouraged to cluster objects in equal groups to more easily find the total.

9

Estimate and Measure

CONTENT AREA

Measurement

Number and
Operations

MATERIALS

■ optional: overhead
projector

TIME

five to fifteen minutes

Overview

Measurement is an often overlooked part of the math curriculum.
Typically the topic is relegated to the last chapters of the math book, and
students merely receive a quick overview in preparation for a standardized
test. Sadly, many children today do not get measurement experiences outside of school. Even in the upper-elementary grades, students lack experience with rulers and are unfamiliar with the different measurement types
and purposes. *Estimate and Measure* gives students different measurement
experiences throughout the entire school year.

Activity Directions

1. Ask students to estimate the number of paces it will take you to cross
   the length of the classroom.
2. Record the estimates on the board or an overhead.
3. With the class, determine the range of the estimates.
4. Discuss the estimates and have several volunteers explain their thinking.
5. Walk the length of the room as the students count your paces. Ask students whether the actual measurement is within their range of estimates.
6. Repeat Steps 1 through 5, this time using the width of the classroom.
7. Introduce the term *linear* and its meaning.
8. Have students generate a class list of things to measure using linear
   measurement.
9. Have students generate their own written questions about things to
   estimate and measure.

Key Questions

- How did you decide on your estimate?
- What did you consider that helped you think about it?
- Can you use the information that you already have to help you make
  another estimate?

From the Classroom

I wasn't sure how much measurement experience Melissa Mechtly's third graders already had, so I decided to focus on linear measurement first.

"I've been in your classroom a bunch of times," I told the class. "But I usually just stay up here by the rug. I want to spend today's session getting to know the space better. So the first thing I'm wondering about is how many steps it would take me to walk across the room."

"Which way?" Omar asked.

The classroom was in a portable trailer that was significantly rectangular in shape. Omar wanted to know if I would be traveling the length or width of the room. This was a perfect opportunity to introduce some measurement vocabulary in context.

"Good question," I responded. "I think I'll walk the length of the room, from the whiteboard all the way back to the sink. That's the longer way. Maybe I'll walk the width of the room after. To walk the width of the room, I'd need to go from the door all the way across to the bulletin boards."

I gestured with my arms to clarify which parts of the room I was referring to. On the board I wrote:

Length of Room Estimates

"OK," I continued, "let's hear some of your estimates for the number of steps I'll take when I walk across the room. Remember, it's an estimate, so you're making a thoughtful mathematical guess. I don't even know what the answer is yet. The important part of estimating is thinking mathematically. Good estimates help you decide if your answer is reasonable. Think for a moment and then I'll give a signal for you to just say your answers aloud. I'll record all the ideas on the board."

I had students "popcorn" their estimates as I wrote them on the board. The popcorn approach allows students to call out answers in rapid succession as I record them. I wanted to minimize the risk to individuals and encourage all students to participate. This approach also quickly yielded many data to discuss. In less than thirty seconds, the board was full of estimates.

Length of Room Estimates

20	15	25	40	21	10
22	20	60	15	16	30
18	45	12	25	14	18

I started with a few general questions and then I moved on to individual sharing. "What's the lowest estimate and the highest estimate?" I asked.

"Ten is the lowest and sixty is the highest," Vincent responded.

"OK," I said, "these two numbers can help us find the range of estimates. How many numbers are there between ten and sixty?"

"Fifty," several students answered almost immediately.

"OK," I said, "so the range of your estimates is fifty."

"Let's hear about your thinking," I moved on. "Is there anyone willing to tell us how you decided on your estimate? What kinds of things did you consider that helped you come up with a number?"

"Well," Tyrone explained, "I thought about how big your steps are and I pictured you walking across the room."

"I did it a different way," Terry offered. "I thought about how many steps it would take you to go halfway across the room. Then I doubled it."

After hearing from several other students, I took the actual measurement. I started at one end of the room and walked across to the other end. I had the students count each step aloud to keep them all involved and focused. We established that it took twenty-two steps for me to walk the length of the room.

"So you know the length of the room is twenty-two of my steps," I noted. "Was the actual number of steps within the range of your estimates?"

"Yes," Antoinette responded, "because our estimates were between ten and sixty."

"OK," I continued, "now you're going to think about how wide the room is, or its width. Can you use the information you already know about the length of the room to estimate the width of the room? Talk to a partner and then we'll listen to your ideas."

I gave the students some time to discuss this new question. Most of them compared the length of the room with the width and adjusted their estimates accordingly. We repeated the *Estimate and Measure* procedure, this time measuring the width of the room.

"When we measure the length or the width of something, it's called *linear measurement*," I told the class as I wrote *linear* on the board. "Does anyone see a word within that word that can give you a hint about what it means?"

"Ear!" Pilar noted enthusiastically.

"Well, yes," I acknowledged, somewhat surprised. "I didn't notice that before, but there it is. Any other words you see in there?"

"In," Kristin noticed.

"Good," I replied. "What else?"

"Line?" John offered.

"Yes," I responded, "*Line* is in *linear*. That tells us that when we're doing linear measurement we're measuring a line. When I walked the length of the room I measured a line across the room. Anytime we measure a line, whether it's horizontal, vertical, or diagonal, we are doing linear measurement. What other linear measure could we do in this room?"

"We can measure the door," Javier suggested.

"Yes," I agreed as I walked over to the door, "we could measure the height of the door or the width of the door."

"But how could you walk up the door?" Terry challenged.

"Good point," I responded. "Since I don't have my antigravity boots on, it would be pretty difficult for me to walk up the door. Are there any tools I could use to measure the height of the door?"

"You could use a ruler," Mia suggested.

"Or a tape measure," Ignacio added.

"Or a yardstick," Hakim pointed out.

"Great," I responded. "You know about a lot of measurement tools. These tools are very helpful for two reasons. First, they keep me from having to defy gravity. Even more important, when we use these standard tools, everyone knows what we're talking about. If you went home and told your family that your classroom is twenty-two Caren steps long, they wouldn't necessarily know how long the room is because they don't know how big my steps are. But if you told them the measurement in feet or yards, they could have a pretty good sense of it."

I refocused the discussion on linear measurement possibilities. The students generated a list of things in the classroom that they could measure. The list included things such as the rug, a book, a window, a desk, and the calendar. Then we talked about different tools in the classroom that we could use to do the measuring. This list included standard and nonstandard measuring tools such as rulers, markers, pattern blocks, pencils, and yardsticks. Satisfied that the students had enough ideas, I sent them back to their tables to write down some *Estimate and Measure* ideas in their journals. The students had many ideas, such as How many pencils long is my desk? How many inches across is the sink? and How tall is the classroom in feet? These student-generated suggestions would be used for future *Estimate and Measure* opportunities.

Extending the Activity

A lot of measurement practice and concept development happen through repeated *Estimate and Measure* experiences. I used a nonstandard measurement (my footsteps) to introduce the activity. The nonstandard unit was less formal and allowed students to feel safe in their initial estimating task. Using standard measurement units such as inches, feet, or centimeters helps students get a feel for the size of these units. It also provides opportunities to use measuring tools and record measurements using proper notation.

The focus can shift to other types of measurement as well. The same procedure can be used to focus on area, surface area, volume and capacity, or weight.

Estimation Jar

10

Overview

Estimation Jar delivers a lot of math in a short period of time. In this activity, students make estimates about the contents of a jar. By offering visual models of quantities, this activity helps students build their number sense. It is important to emphasize the thinking involved in making estimates rather than which estimate is right or closest. Over time students begin to use more sophisticated approaches to making estimates and determining reasonableness.

Activity Directions

1. Fill a clear container with objects (e.g, counters, cubes, or cotton balls).
2. Have students estimate how many objects they think are in the jar.
3. Record the estimates on the board or an overhead.
4. Have a few students share their thought processes in coming up with their estimates.
5. Provide a benchmark for each group or table of students, such as a handful of ten objects.
6. Discuss how the benchmark helps them think about their estimates.
7. Ask students to determine the number of objects you removed from the jar. Have students share their calculation strategies.
8. Ask students how many objects they think are still in the jar and how this information helps them with their estimate of the total number of objects.
9. Continue distributing handfuls of ten objects to each of the groups, each time determining the number of objects outside the jar.
10. Repeat Step 9 until you run out of handfuls of ten. Then count the objects remaining in the jar.
11. Have students determine how many objects were in the jar altogether and share their computation strategies.

CONTENT AREA

Number and Operations

MATERIALS

- clear jar or container (an empty olive or peanut butter jar works well)
- cubes, beans, marbles, or other objects, enough to fill the jar
- optional: overhead projector

TIME

ten to fifteen minutes

Key Questions

- What did you do or look at that helped you make an estimate?
- How many objects are out? How many objects do you think are still in?
- How does the new information change your ideas?

From the Classroom

I began the *Estimation Jar* activity by showing a group of fifth-grade students a jar I had filled with color tiles. I asked them to make an estimate of how many color tiles they thought were in the jar. I reminded them that they couldn't know exactly how many tiles there were, so their thinking was the important part, not whether they were right or closest. This is an important message for students. Often they experience estimation jars as a contest rather than a math activity. I wanted to keep the focus on the students' thinking and off the stress of a competition.

After giving students a few moments to think, I asked for volunteers to share their estimates. I recorded the estimates on the board.

"We've got quite a range of estimates here," I told the class. "I wonder why. Is anyone willing to talk about what you did or looked at that helped you make an estimate?"

Several students raised their hands and I called on Nadine.

"I was looking at the jar and thinking about how much it would take to fill it," she explained.

"I looked at how big the jar is," Tyler added.

"You also should think about how small the tiles are," Quoc contributed.

These short conversations are extremely valuable as they provide models of thinking for the entire class.

"OK," I told the class. "I'm going to give you a benchmark that might help you think about your estimates. Is it OK to change your estimate when you have more information?"

The class agreed that it was. I went around the room and put ten tiles from the jar in the middle of each of the four tables in the room.

"Now you can see what ten tiles looks like. How does this new information change your ideas?" I asked.

Miguel explained, "We can see how much space ten tiles fill and we can figure out how much space there is in the jar."

"Or we can just picture putting in bunches of ten to see how many fit," Rashad offered.

After allowing the students to contemplate the use of their benchmark tiles, I shifted gears and asked them how many tiles were out of the jar at the moment. It was fairly easy for them to tell me that there were forty out, but I wanted to check for understanding and different thought processes. I asked how they knew I had removed forty tiles from the jar, and I got two different explanations. One student said that $10 + 10 + 10 + 10 = 40$. Another student said $10 \times 4 = 40$. We took a moment to talk about how these two equations were equivalent and how they connected to the tiles on the tables. Then we moved back to the estimation jar.

I held up the jar so everyone could see. "So we know there are forty tiles out of the jar right now," I told the class. "How many tiles do you think are still in here and how does that help you with your estimate?"

"We took forty out and that was about twenty-five percent," Marshall replied.

"That's the same as one-fourth," Miguel commented.

Denise jumped on the percent bandwagon. "I'd say there's about sixty-five percent of the jar still full," she offered.

"There's three-quarters left," Dolly posited, "and we have forty out, so it's going to be about one hundred five."

Despite Dolly's miscalculation, I was pleased that students were using fractions and percents to describe the situation. I decided not to push this aspect of the discussion at this point because I wanted to make sure all students stayed engaged and focused on the estimating. I made a mental note to revisit the fraction and percent ideas in future estimation tasks. Nakesha brought the conversation back to the tiles in the jar.

"My new estimate is one hundred forty-four," she explained, "because if we took ten more out of the jar there would be fifty out altogether. Then if we took another fifty out there would be about forty-four left. So that would be one forty-four."

"I counted the forty we have on the tables and then I looked at all the tiles I could see on the inside of the jar," Kevin explained. "It looks like about seventy-six."

At this point I put another ten tiles on each table and repeated the sequence of questions. I asked how many tiles were out of the jar, how they knew, and how many they thought were left in the jar. We did two more rounds of putting ten tiles on each table, so then each table had a total of forty tiles. We estimated that there weren't enough tiles to give each table another ten. I dumped out the remaining tiles and counted them with the students. We established that there were twelve tiles left. My final question to the students was "How many tiles were in the jar altogether?" The students had all the numerical information needed to figure it out. I gave them about a minute to do the computation and then had several students share their strategies with the class.

Randi pointed to two tables and said, "Forty plus forty is eighty. The other two tables make another eighty. Eighty plus eighty is one sixty. One hundred sixty plus twelve equals one seventy-two." I wrote Randi's idea on the board.

40 + 40 = 80
80 + 80 = 160
160 + 12 = 172

Marshall multiplied the number of tables by the number of tiles at each table. Then he added the remaining twelve tiles to find the total. I recorded his strategy on the board.

40 × 4 = 160
160 + 12 = 172

Estimation Jar proved to be a rich experience. It gave students opportunities to speak, listen, estimate, and do mental computation. Over time the students would become even more adept at combining their number sense with computation in order to make reasonable estimates in a variety of contexts.

Extending the Activity

There are many ways to modify the *Estimation Jar* activity. The modifications not only help keep the activity fresh, but also give students multiple models for estimation and computation. One simple idea is to keep the contents (in this case color tiles) the same and use a different-size or different-shape jar. In this way students can still use the benchmark quantities but apply them to a different space. Conversely, you can fill the original jar with a different item (e.g., use marbles instead of color tiles) to allow students to consider the relative proportions of the objects and apply them to a constant container.

Another option is to begin with an empty jar and have students estimate as you gradually fill it with benchmark quantities (e.g., add ten tiles to the jar and have students estimate how many will fill the jar, then add more to get to fifty, have them estimate again, and so on). Some teachers have their students take ownership of a weekly estimation jar. Students are assigned the task on a rotating basis. Each week the selected student is responsible for bringing in a filled estimation jar from home. This fosters home-school connections and honors the items that students have in their home environments.

Function Machine

11

Overview

During the *Function Machine* activity, students look at pairs of numbers and try to generalize relationships and patterns. They also use mathematical language to describe the relationships and to connect the relationships to math vocabulary and symbols. *Function Machine* is a fun and flexible way to encourage communication and algebraic thinking. It also provides a context for introducing and using some of the tools of algebra, such as T-charts.

CONTENT AREA

Algebra

Number and Operations

MATERIALS

- optional: overhead projector

TIME

ten minutes

Activity Directions

1. Draw a "machine" on the board or an overhead. See the example below.

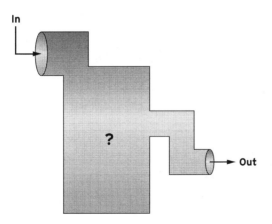

2. Tell students when a number is put into your machine, the machine follows a certain rule to produce the Out number (e.g., add three). Their job is to figure out the machine's rule.
3. Remind students of the importance of not yelling out the rule the machine is following when they think they've figured it out.

4. Draw a T-chart and label the columns *In* and *Out*.

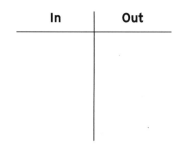

Explain to the students that the T-chart is a way to keep track of what the machine is doing.

5. Have students tell you a number to put into the machine.
6. Record the number on the T-chart in the In column.
7. Tell students what number would come out. Record that number under the Out column.
8. Continue to add students' suggestions for the In number to the T-chart, record the resulting Out numbers, and have students look for patterns and discuss what the machine might be doing to the numbers.
9. Add a twist by giving the students an Out number and asking them to figure out what number went in.
10. Have students describe what they think the rule is.
11. Record their ideas on the board.

Key Questions

- What do you notice about the numbers on the T-chart?
- What might this function machine be doing?

From the Classroom

Danielle Pickett introduced the *Function Machine* activity to her third graders by drawing an odd-looking tubular machine on the board. The picture piqued their curiosity and she immediately had their attention.

"This," she explained to the class, "is a function machine. A number goes into my function machine, my function machine does something to the In number, and a new number comes out. The function machine always does the same thing to the In number until you guess the rule. Your job is to guess what my machine is doing to the In numbers."

The students seemed excited to get started.

"There are a couple of things you need to know first," Danielle told them. "After you put some numbers into the machine and see what comes out, you'll start to have an idea of what my function machine is doing. It's going to be really important that you don't shout out the answer. We want to make sure everyone in the class has a chance to think as much as possible. OK?"

The students agreed.

"However," she told the class, "if you do think you know what the function machine is doing, you can test out your idea without shouting it out. You can put numbers in and see if you can predict what will come out."

Danielle felt it was important to get these ground rules out in the open at the beginning of the activity. In all classes there is a range of learners and some students are quick to come up with answers or ideas they want to share. When those students always jump in with their thoughts, it has some negative effects on other students. First, the students who need more time to think get discouraged. Second, some students stop thinking altogether because they know someone else will just say the answer for them.

The flip side of this dilemma is that students who do have answers and ideas need to be encouraged. That's why it's important to give them something to do with their ideas other than shout them out. Meeting the needs of a wide range of learners is one of the biggest challenges in teaching whole-class math lessons. Making sure everyone has access to the activity is crucial. For a function machine, a student just needs to be able to suggest a number in order to get involved. This makes the entry point accessible for all students. So two key questions to consider when planning whole-class math lessons are What's the baseline entry point for all students? and What is the challenge or extension for this activity?

Danielle then drew a T-chart on the board, labeling the columns *In* and *Out*. Danielle said to her class, "This chart will help us keep track of the In and Out numbers and help us see what's happening with the numbers. Who would like to give me a number to put into the function machine?"

Many students waved their hands in the air. Danielle called on Carol, knowing that she was an English language learner who was being brave enough to speak in front of the whole class. Even though Carol would be saying only one number, it would help bolster her confidence and encourage her to take more risks in the future.

"Seven?" Carol tried.

"Well," Danielle responded as she wrote on the T-chart, "if a seven goes in, a ten comes out."

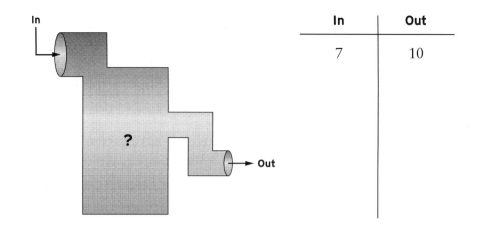

In	Out
7	10

"Ooooh!" Amir exclaimed. "I know what it's doing."

"Careful though," Danielle cautioned. "Sometimes you need more information or data before you know exactly what's going on. Also, please don't shout out the machine's rule, as this will stop people's thinking. Does someone want to try a different In number?"

"Put a nine in," Janetta suggested.

"Nine goes in, twelve comes out," the teacher told Janetta while recording the numbers in the chart. "Anyone else?"

"How about three?" John volunteered.

"When a three goes in, a six comes out," Danielle told him.

At this point Danielle could tell many of the students had an idea of what the function machine was doing. She decided to mix things up a bit to keep them involved while giving others more time and more information.

"Nod your head if you think you know what my function machine is doing," she said to the class.

Most students nodded.

"Look at the T-chart," she told the class. "What do you notice about the numbers?"

The students looked a bit confused and hesitant, so Danielle asked a more specific question. "Are the Out numbers greater or less than the In numbers?"

"Greater," the class responded.

"So let's think about this function machine. What operations could it be using that would make a number bigger?"

"Addition," Vincent suggested.

"Or multiplication," Claudia added.

"True," Danielle agreed. "Do the Out numbers get a lot bigger or a little bit bigger?"

"A little," Josue replied.

"So does that tell you anything about the operation the function machine might be using?"

"It's addition, because when you multiply a number it usually gets a lot bigger," Kanani observed.

"Not always," John objected. "Like if you multiply by one or zero, the number stays the same or gets smaller."

"Good point," Danielle acknowledged. "Also, we're using positive whole numbers. Negative numbers or fractions or decimals don't always get bigger when you add or multiply with them."

Danielle was pleased with this brief exchange. She had wanted to bring some of the effects of operations to the surface of the discussion so students would begin to think about them in terms of the *Function Machine*. The discussion also allowed Danielle a chance to refer to negative numbers and fractions, reminding students that it's a big world of numbers out there and they needed to be careful not to overgeneralize. She decided to move on, still using the same rule.

"Now," she told the students, "I'm going to make it a little trickier. This time I'm going to tell you what came out and you need to tell me what went in."

She wrote *8* in the Out column.

"Talk to a neighbor sitting near you. What went in that caused eight to come out? Make sure you really explain your thinking so you understand each other."

Danielle gave the students some time to talk. This talk served two purposes. It allowed students to clarify and verbalize their ideas about the function machine. It also gave students who hadn't yet figured out the function an opportunity to hear others talk about it.

"So what do you think?" she asked the class. "What went into the machine?"

"Five," Kanani said with confidence.

"Rats!" Danielle said, "I thought I could trick you, but you're right. OK, I'm going to try an even harder one. What if I told you twenty-one came out? Talk to a neighbor about what went in."

Danielle deliberately picked a higher number so that the students would do some mental computation. While it's important to introduce the function machine with numbers and operations that are easily accessible, once the students catch on, there are opportunities to have them do some more challenging computation in the context of the machine. She called for the students' attention and asked for a volunteer to give her the In number. She wrote *18* on the T-chart after Terrell shared it.

"All right," Danielle said to the now very confident group, "I can see you're ready for the ultimate challenge. What if I told you that two came out? This is super challenging, so talk to a neighbor and see what you think."

Although these third graders had had minimal exposure to negative numbers, Danielle was curious to see how they might handle this problem. She eavesdropped on the students' conversations. Some students were stuck on zero as the only possibility, but the idea of negative one started to circulate. She called on Sally.

"Negative one," Sally exclaimed.

"Wow," Danielle responded as she wrote -1 on the chart. "How did you figure that out?"

"It's because you have to go back three," Sally explained. "And if you're at two and you go back three, you pass zero and get to negative one."

"Makes sense to me," Danielle agreed. "So let's talk about this function machine. What does it do to numbers? Let's see how many different ways you can find to explain it. Raise your hand if you have a way to describe what the function machine does." She called on Antonio.

"It adds three to the number," he said.

Danielle wrote on the board:

Add three

"Is there another way to describe it?" Danielle asked.

"Plus three," Marta contributed.

Danielle wrote *Plus three* on the board and asked for other ways.

"Take away three," Nikki said.

"Hmm," Danielle responded, "I guess that's true if you look at the Out number first. Let me think of a way to write that." She wrote on the board:

Out number − 3 = In number

"Does that work?" she asked the class.

The students nodded in agreement.

"So can I also write this?" Danielle asked.

In number + 3 = Out number

"Yes," the class replied.

"So there are a lot of ways to describe what this function machine does," Danielle summarized. "I'm impressed with all your thinking today. You've gotten so good at this, maybe you can think of some function machines and I can try to guess them next time." The children were excited by the idea and looked forward to creating their own function machines.

Extending the Activity

Function Machine is very adaptable. Start with a fairly simple function (e.g., +3). Depending on students' levels and area of study, any numbers and operations could be used. Also, you might choose to use a combination of numbers and operations (e.g., ×2 + 1). As students become familiar with function machines, they can start to make up their own rules. Students can then take on the teacher role, leading the activity. It's a good idea to have children prepare their own T-charts for the In numbers from zero to twenty along with the resulting Out numbers. Check the chart prior to having a student share his or her rule. This prevents errors and embarrassment. It also speeds up the process, keeping all students on task. Of course this means that students must suggest numbers from zero to twenty when trying to guess the rule.

Function Machine can also easily be connected to coordinate graphing. The coordinate pairs generated on the T-chart can be plotted on a graph. Students can then discuss what they notice about the graph and how it's related to the function.

12

CONTENT AREA

Number and
Operations

MATERIALS

■ optional: overhead
projector

TIME

five to ten minutes

Guess My Number

Overview

Guess My Number invites children to consider the structure of the number system while engaging in a logic game. Students try to guess a secret number from within a given range of possibilities. *Guess My Number* also presents an opportunity to reinforce mathematical symbols such as the "greater than" and "less than" signs. Through *Guess My Number,* students find the usefulness of number lines as tools for solving problems.

Activity Directions

1. Choose a number between a given range (e.g., 1–10, 1–20, 500–1,000). Draw a number line on the board or an overhead to represent the range.
2. Tell the students, "I'm thinking of a number between __ and __. Who has a guess?"
3. Elicit guesses from the students, responding each time with a clue. For example, if a student guesses fifteen, tell the class whether your number is greater than or less than fifteen.
4. Record the guesses and your responses on the board.
5. Ask students to explain why their guesses make sense.
6. When the students have narrowed down the possible secret numbers, ask them to discuss with a partner the following: what they already know about the secret number and what next guess they would like to make.
7. Lead a brief discussion for students to share their thinking and then continue to take guesses until the students discover the secret number.

Key Questions

- What do you know already about my number?
- How does that guess help you?

From the Classroom

Patty Stark's fifth graders had just started their Tuesday morning. As they settled into their seats, I went to the board and drew a box with a question mark inside it.

"Good morning," I greeted the class. "I've got a secret number for you to guess. Since it's early in the morning I'm going to make it pretty easy for you. I'll tell you the number is somewhere between one and one hundred."

"Could it be one hundred?" Martina asked.

"Yes," I responded. "It could be any number between one and one hundred, including one or one hundred. You can guess a number and I'll tell you if my secret number is greater than or less than your guess."

I drew a number line on the board to help the students keep track of their guesses.

"How about fifty?" Latoya asked.

"The secret number is less than fifty," I told her as I wrote this information on the board. I also marked 50 on the number line with an arrow indicating all the numbers fifty and above were too large.

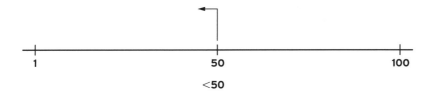

Before I took any more guesses I decided to have a brief discussion about strategies for guessing. I had deliberately picked an easy number to start with so we could focus on the mechanics and thinking involved with the game.

"I'm a bit curious, Latoya," I said. "Is there a particular reason you chose fifty?"

"Yeah," Latoya responded. "I knew your number was between one and one hundred, so I picked fifty because it's in the middle."

"So how does that guess help you?" I pushed.

"Because it splits the numbers. Since you said the secret number is less than fifty, I know it's in the bottom half of the numbers."

I summarized Latoya's strategy with accompanying references to the number line. "I think I get it," I told the class. "All the possible numbers are between one and one hundred. So if you guess a number right in the middle, you can figure out which half the secret number is in and then you can just throw away the other half and not have to worry about it."

I proceeded to take some more guesses. Within a minute the number line looked like this:

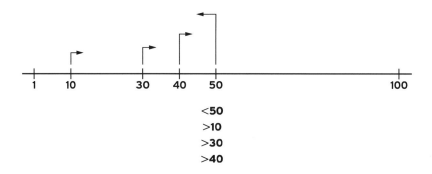

<50
>10
>30
>40

I decided to encourage some partner talk. I had students pair up and briefly discuss two things—what they thought they already knew about my secret number and what number they'd like to guess next. I wrote the two prompts on the board to help them stay focused. Also, I was giving them a preview of the discussion to come.

What do you already know about my secret number?
What next guess would you like to make? Why?

After a few minutes I called for the students' attention. "So can anyone tell something you know about my secret number?" I asked.

"It's more than forty," Hilario offered.

"It's between forty and fifty," David added.

"It's in the forties," Brenda posited.

"So you already know a lot about the secret number," I validated. "So with all this information, what number would you like to guess next? If you raise your hand to guess a number, you also have to be willing to explain why you think that number is a helpful guess."

I called on Destinee.

"Forty-five," she volunteered.

"Why is forty-five helpful?" I asked.

"Because," Destinee explained, "we know the secret number is in the forties and forty-five is in the middle of the forties."

"It's just like Latoya's idea," Reynaldo chimed in. "You can get rid of half the numbers that are left."

"Aha," I responded, "so you're using your logical thinking to help eliminate a bunch of possibilities with one guess. Well, I'll tell you that the secret number is less than forty-five. Talk to a partner again about what you know about the number now and what guess you'd like to make next."

I let the students talk to each other as I added the new information to the number line. Many students wanted to use the same strategy and pick the number that was halfway between forty and forty-five. We took a brief detour to establish that 42.5 was the midpoint between forty and forty-five, but I explained that this *Guess My Number* game involved whole numbers only, so they needed to choose either forty-two or forty-three.

Christina guessed forty-two. I told her that the secret number was greater than forty-two and recorded this information on the board. Then Kenny guessed forty-nine. Some students expressed frustration with his guess since they already knew the number was less than forty-five. I stopped briefly to have a talk about maintaining a safe environment.

"This is a new game we're playing today," I told the class. "Part of learning and trying new things is making mistakes. It's really important that everyone in the class feels safe enough to share his or her ideas and sometimes make mistakes. That's how we learn. If you disagree with someone or you have a different idea, that's fine. Just make sure you communicate that in a way that won't hurt anyone's feelings. Do you know what I'm talking about?" I asked the class as I looked at each student.

"Yes," the students murmured.

I added Kenny's guess to the board and moved on.

"How about forty-three?" Lisa suggested.

I wrote *43* on the board and circled it.

"Yes," I congratulated. "My number is forty-three. I'm impressed with everyone's thinking. It could have been any of one hundred different numbers, and it took you only eight guesses to get it. That shows you used a lot of good mathematical thinking."

Before I left the class, I called on a pair of students to lead the class in another round of *Guess My Number.*

Extending the Activity

Guess My Number works equally well with fractions, decimals, or percents. Giving the students some visual tools is essential. Using a number line helps students compare numbers and order the numbers.

A 1–100 chart is another tool that works nicely for *Guess My Number.* Tell students that the secret number is somewhere on the 1–100 chart.

Cross numbers off the chart as they are eliminated. Familiarity with a 1–100 chart gives upper-elementary students a distinctive edge when it comes to mental computation and understanding our number system. When students have a visual model of the chart in their heads, they can easily jump around using tens. They also have a useful geometric model (the 10-by-10 square) to get a feel for how numbers are related to one another. Playing *Guess My Number* with a 1–100 chart gives students further exposure to the chart and pushes them to articulate some of the number relationships inherent in it.

Guess My Rule

13

CONTENT AREA

Number and Operations

Geometry

MATERIALS

■ optional: overhead
  projector

TIME

five to ten minutes

Overview

Guess My Rule is a highly adaptable game that encourages children to consider attributes of numbers and sort and classify them. Students make guesses about a secret rule relating to numbers using a Venn diagram as a visual model. The teacher puts the students' guesses in the appropriate section of the Venn. As the sections of the Venn fill with information, students look for patterns and relationships to discern the rules that might apply.

Activity Directions

1. Choose a rule (e.g., odd numbers, multiples of three, prime numbers).
2. Draw a circle on the board or an overhead and explain the activity to the students. Remind them not to shout out the rule when they have figured it out.
3. Ask a student to tell you a number.
4. Put the number in the circle if it fits your rule. Put it outside the circle if it doesn't fit your rule.
5. Continue eliciting numbers and placing them in the appropriate area.
6. After recording several numbers, have students discuss the information they have so far.
7. Ask students for numbers that will either go inside the circle or go outside.
8. Ask the class to state the rule.
9. Repeat the activity with two different rules about numbers and a two-circle Venn diagram.

Key Questions

- What do you notice about the numbers inside the circle?
- What is the next number you want to try?
- Can anyone tell me a number that you think belongs inside/outside the circle?
- If I told you a number, could you tell me where to put it?

From the Classroom

I started *Guess My Rule* with Patty Stark's fifth graders in a simple format. Prior to beginning the activity, I chose an easy secret rule—odd numbers. To begin the activity, I drew a large box on the board and drew a circle inside it.

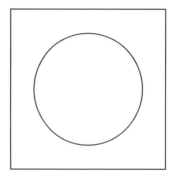

"OK," I told the class, "I've got a secret rule about numbers. You are going to tell me a number. If that number fits my rule, I'll put it inside the circle. If it doesn't fit the rule, I'll write it outside the circle. After a while there will be a bunch of numbers up here and you'll start to notice things about the numbers that might give you clues about my rule. Here's something important." I paused for emphasis.

"If you think you know the secret rule, *don't* shout it out. We want to give everyone in the class enough time to think about it. If someone shouts out the answer, it cuts off everyone else's thinking. Get it?"

I surveyed the room with my serious face.

"Good," I moved on. "Raise your hand if you'd like to give me a number."

"Nine," Timothy offered.

"Nine goes inside the circle," I replied as I wrote 9 inside the Venn diagram.

"How about three?" Aja suggested.

"Three goes inside the circle as well," I told her.

I took several more numbers and added them to the board.

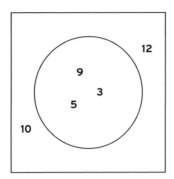

I stopped the number sharing and had the students refocus on the information they already had.

"Here's what I'm going to do," I told the class as I looked at my watch. "I'm going to give you forty-seven seconds to talk to people at your table about what you're thinking about the secret rule and what next number you might want to try. Ready, go."

Using a short time limit forces students to get right to the point. There's some psychological component to having an odd number of seconds in which to complete a task or discussion; students seem to rise to the occasion and get to work quickly. Maybe it's just the strangeness of the situation, but whatever it is, it works.

I made an ostentatious show of keeping track of the time. When the time was up, I called for the class's attention.

"Time's up," I announced. "I'm curious to know what you're thinking at this point, but I don't want to anyone to say the answer yet. You can show me with your thumbs. Put you thumb up if you think you know the rule. Put your thumb down if you don't know the rule. Put your thumb to the side if you're not sure."

Almost all the students had their thumbs up, so I tried a new twist to keep the game interesting both for those who knew and those who needed a little more time.

"Well," I prompted, "if you think you know the rule, tell me a number that fits inside the circle."

Many hands shot up. I called on Jessica.

"Eleven," she said.

"Yes," I agreed, "eleven fits the rule."

"So does twenty-seven," Victor added.

"Right again," I responded. "Can anyone tell me a number that goes outside the circle?"

"Fifty," Jasmin volunteered.

"Good," I said. "Now how about this challenge: I'm looking for a three-digit number that goes outside the circle."

"Four hundred fifty-two," Alejandro suggested.

"Great," I responded as I wrote the number on the board. "How about a four-digit number that fits outside the circle?"

"One thousand seven hundred sixty-two," Marvin volunteered.

"Wow," I said, "it seems like you've figured out the rule. If I told you a number, would you be able to tell me whether it goes inside or outside the circle?"

Heads were nodding around the room. Many students had raised their hands, each eager to be the one to say the rule. I diffused the situation by allowing everyone to be the hero.

"Here's what's going to happen," I told the class. "I'm going to count to three. After I say 'three,' you say the rule in a quiet voice. Ready? One, two, three."

"Odd numbers," the students chorused.

"You got it," I confirmed. "Now I think you're ready for the challenging level."

I drew a large rectangle on the board and drew two overlapping circles inside it.

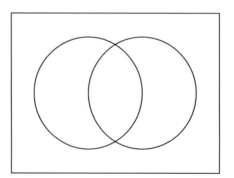

"This time I've got two secret rules," I explained. I pointed to the different sections of the Venn I had created. (I had decided to use multiples of three for one rule and even numbers for the other rule.)

"Some numbers you say will fit one rule, some will fit the other rule, some will fit both rules, and some will fit neither rule."

I followed the same sequence I had done with the single-rule version. Individuals told me numbers and I wrote them in the appropriate area. After a few minutes, the board looked like this:

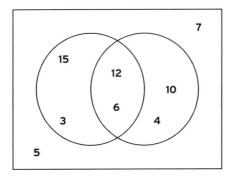

I had the students stop and talk at their tables for fifty-three seconds. (I'm telling you, it works.) Then I called them back together for a brief discussion.

"I noticed that there were all even numbers on the right and all the numbers outside were odd," Jessica pointed out.

"But the numbers on the left side are odd, too," Caleb pointed out.

"The ones on the left are counting by threes," Ana observed.

"They're the multiples of three," Eric elaborated.

"Yes, that was one of my rules," I told the class as I labeled the circle on the left.

"What about this other circle?" I asked. "What do you think the rule is for this one?"

"Those are even numbers," Phillip observed.

"Yup," I agreed as I labeled the other circle. "So what about these numbers in the middle?"

"They fit both. They're even and they're multiples of three," Stacie explained.

I confirmed Stacie's assertion. I thanked the students for their work and their thinking. I left feeling that *Guess My Rule* was both an engaging and a mathematically worthwhile activity that could easily be modified and revisited throughout the year.

Extending the Activity

Guess My Rule is a very malleable activity. You might introduce the activity using only one rule, but then increase the challenge by using two or even three rules simultaneously. Once students are familiar with the format of the game, they can make up their own rules and lead class games. When using more than one rule, make sure the rules have some overlapping possibilities and are not mutually exclusive (e.g., odd numbers and even numbers wouldn't work because there's nothing that would go in the overlapping section).

Guess My Rule translates extremely well to geometry. Use rules about shapes or other geometric attributes. The activity also works well with concrete materials. Buttons, pattern blocks, even people can be physically sorted. Students can use the visual models to ascertain the similarities and discover the secret rules.

Guess My Rule can also be easily integrated into other curricular areas. In a science unit on animals, for example, a *Guess My Rule* game can feature mammals and animals that live in trees. In history or social science, it can be used to compare states, countries, or cultures. In any context, *Guess My Rule* helps students develop the problem-solving, reasoning, and communication skills that are integral parts of the NCTM Standards.

How Far Away?

14

Overview

In this activity students use the benchmark number of one hundred to explore other numbers and their relation to one hundred. This activity also gives students opportunities to employ their understanding of place value and practice mental computation. Modeling the use of a number line provides students with a visual tool for computation. In addition, the explicit use of benchmark numbers (twenty-five, fifty, seventy-five, one hundred) encourages students to connect unfamiliar problems with ones they already know.

Activity Directions

1. Roll three dice or have students roll the dice. If more than one roll is the same, roll a die again until you have three different numbers to work with.
2. Record the results of the rolls on the board or an overhead.
3. Tell students to make all the possible two-digit numbers with the rolls and record them on board.
4. Create a 0–100 number line and have students help you locate the benchmark numbers 25, 50, and 75 on it.
5. Have students discuss in pairs where their two-digit numbers should go on the number line. Then ask for volunteers to tell you how to place the numbers.
6. Ask students which number is closest to 100 and which is farthest away.
7. Have them use the number line to compute how close and how far away each of the numbers is from 100. Ask students to share their thinking and record their strategies on the board.

Key Questions

- How far away from one hundred is this number?
- How can you use what you know about benchmark numbers to help you?

CONTENT AREA

Number and Operations

MATERIALS

- optional: overhead projector
- 3 dice

TIME

ten minutes

From the Classroom

I introduced *How Far Away?* to Melissa Mechtly's third graders by telling them I'd heard a lot about how much they liked math and what great thinkers they were. "So I thought you'd be the perfect class to try a new game," I continued.

"We love math games!" Charlie informed me.

"Great," I replied. "Then let's get started. I brought some dice with me today. In lots of games you roll one or two. For this game I'm going to roll three."

A murmur of excitement spread across the room.

"Yes," I acknowledged, "it's a pretty special game and that's why I wanted to find the right class to share it with."

"So here's how it works," I continued. "I'm going to roll the three dice and record the results on the board. You're going to try to find all the different two-digit numbers you can make with the numbers I rolled. What do I mean by a two-digit number?"

"Like twelve," Reggie offered.

"Yes," I agreed. "Twelve is a two-digit number. What are some other two-digit numbers?"

The students shouted out a bunch of numbers. I settled them down and then continued.

"You do know a lot of two-digit numbers," I commented. "Turn to a partner and explain how you can tell if it's a two-digit number or not."

I gave the students less than a minute and then moved on. To begin, I asked three different students to roll a die. When two students rolled 6s I had one roll again because we needed three different numbers. I wrote the numbers on the board.

6   2   4

"So there are your three numbers," I told the class. "Now your job is to make as many two-digit numbers as you can from those numbers. Can anyone think of an example?"

"Sixty-two," Natalie said.

"Yes," I agreed, "we can take the six and the two and make sixty-two. What other numbers can we make?"

It didn't take long for the students to generate all six possibilities, which I recorded on the board. I chose not to have a discussion about probability and combinations at that point, but it would definitely be worthwhile to do so in the future.

"OK," I told the class, "now we've got these six numbers and we want to think about them in terms of a benchmark number, one hundred. Benchmark numbers are friendly numbers that we use and see a lot."

I drew a number line on the board and labeled *0* at one end and *100* at the other. I asked the students where the benchmark numbers 25, 50, and 75 would go and placed them in the appropriate spots.

"So, let's think about these other numbers," I told the students. "Turn to a partner and quietly discuss where you think each of these numbers fits on the number line and explain why you think that. Make sure you really explain your ideas clearly so your partner understands. Also, make sure you're being a polite and active listener if your partner is talking. I'll give you about a minute and a half. Ready? Go."

While the students talked to each other, I circulated and listened to their discussions. Most of their ideas centered on the benchmark numbers we had already labeled and the concepts of more and less. For example, Patricia told her partner that 46 would go close to 50 but to the left of it since it was a little less than 50. When I was satisfied that the students had had sufficient time to accomplish the job, I called for their attention. The students directed my placement of their numbers. I used a different-colored marker to distinguish their numbers from the benchmark numbers. In a few minutes, we had placed all of the numbers on the number line.

I asked the students to identify the number that was farthest away from 100.

"Twenty-four," they shouted in unison.

"How do you know?" I asked.

"Because, look," Jon explained. "It's closer to zero than the other numbers."

"Yeah," Dinora agreed. "Also, it's the lowest number up there."

"OK," I told them, "I'm convinced. Now here's my next question. How far away from one hundred is it? Think for a moment on your own and then I'm going to have you turn to a partner to talk about it. I'm hoping that this number line and the benchmark numbers will help you answer the question. You might want to look at it and talk about it with your partner."

While I wanted the students to feel free to solve the problem in a comfortable way, I didn't want them to fall back on their same old methods without considering the number line as a potential tool. There's always a delicate balance between supporting student autonomy and encouraging students to try new models. A gentle reminder or suggestion can help move children to new ways of thinking about problems without mandating. Also, carefully framing questions can help students focus on the desired concept or strategy. I tried a question. "So who can tell us how you used the number line to help you solve the problem?"

Several hands shot into the air. I called on Janekya. Her response told me she had prior experience using number lines and increments of ten.

"I pictured a number line and I started at twenty-four. I did eight hops of ten."

"Hold on one minute," I requested. "Since our number line doesn't have tens, I'm going to draw a new one so we can see your thinking." I drew an open number line on the board.

"So you started at twenty-four and kept adding tens?" I checked.

"Yes," Janekya responded.

I created a visual model on the number line. I kept the whole class involved by having the students tell me the sum after each addition of ten. Shortly we had a number line that looked like this:

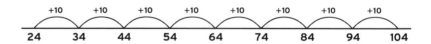

"So what happened when you got to one hundred four?" I queried.

"Well, I knew I was over by four, so I had to take four away from the eighty," she explained.

I wrote $80 - 4 =$ on the board and asked the class for the answer. The students agreed it was 76.

"Did anyone use a number line in a different way to figure out how far twenty-four is from one hundred?" I asked.

Jon volunteered. "I saw that twenty-four was close to twenty-five," he began. "Then I knew twenty-five plus seventy-five is one hundred, so twenty-four is one less than twenty-five, so I gave one to the seventy-five to make it seventy-six."

Although I understood Jon's thinking, I wasn't sure everyone had followed along. "OK," I said, "let me see if I understood you and can put your ideas in my own words."

I referred to our original number line and pointed to the numbers as I talked about them. "You noticed that twenty-four was close to twenty-five. You knew twenty-five plus seventy-five equals one hundred because those are friendly numbers." I wrote on the board:

$$25 + 75 = 100$$

"But," I continued, "this question was about twenty-four, not twenty-five. So you had to think about what number goes with twenty-four to make an equation that totals one hundred." I wrote another equation under the first one.

$$25 + 75 = 100$$
$$24 + \square = 100$$

"Yes," Jon jumped in. "And since twenty-four is one less than twenty-five, I had to give the one to the seventy-five to make it seventy-six."

I pointed to each number as I repeated Jon's explanation of compensation. Then I wrote seventy-six in the box to complete the second equation.

"It's interesting that we heard about two different ways to use a number line to find the difference between two numbers. I'm sure you'll do this activity in the future with your teacher so you'll have even more chances to think about benchmark numbers and use number lines to help you find the differences between numbers," I said to wrap up the activity.

Extending the Activity

Introduce this activity the same way for older students, but once they catch on, change the benchmark to 1,000 and add one more die. Since there are significantly more three-digit number combinations, narrow the focus. Just call on three or four students and have them generate some different three-digit numbers for the class to use. As an alternative, ask the class to use three of the numbers on the dice to make a number that's as far away from 1,000 as possible. They can also try to get as close to 1,000 as possible or try to make numbers that are about 500 away, 250 away, and so on. This reinforces place-value concepts and encourages rounding and estimation.

How Far Away? can also serve as a context for probability investigations. Students can explore how many two-digit numbers can be made with three dice and how many three-digit numbers can be made with four dice.

Looking at Data

15

Overview

In this activity students use graphs to generate and analyze data related to themselves and their surroundings. Graphing activities are excellent routines for upper-elementary students. Regular work with graphs helps students analyze and organize data, think critically, and internalize mathematical vocabulary. A common upper-grade standardized test item involves showing a graph or table and asking students to identify the median, mode, or range. *Looking at Data* reviews these concepts.

Activity Directions

1. Ask students a question that will elicit a range of numerical responses (e.g., How many people live in your home? or What is the last digit of your phone number?). Estimation questions work well, too (e.g., About how many cars are parked outside the school? or About how many teeth are in the classroom?).
2. Use a thick, dark marker to record each student response on its own sticky note.
3. Post the sticky notes randomly on the board as you go.
4. Have students identify the lowest and highest estimate. Place the sticky note with the lowest number at the left end of the board and the sticky note with the highest number at the right end of the board. Then write the numbers on the board as a range (e.g., *171–388*).
5. Ask students to find the range by calculating the difference between the lowest and highest numbers.
6. Let individual students share their approaches as you record on the board using mathematical notation.
7. Have students arrange all the sticky notes in order from lowest to highest so they can find the mode and median.
8. With the students, find the mode and the median.

CONTENT AREA

Data Analysis and Probability

Measurement

MATERIALS

- 3-inch-by-3-inch sticky notes
- a thick, dark marker

TIME

ten to fifteen minutes

Key Questions

- What is the difference between the highest and lowest numbers? How do you know?
- What is the range?
- How can we find the median?
- How can we find the mode?

From the Classroom

I posed a question to the class in order to generate estimates that would become the data for our graph. I had a mixed group of third through fifth graders so I chose a question that would be accessible to the younger students while delivering some intrigue to the older ones.

"If I started at the front door and walked all the way around the perimeter of the school, about how many cars would I find parked on the street?" I asked.

Two sides of the school were bordered by streets. From the classroom window students could see one side of the school's perimeter lined with cars. Many started from there, counting the visible cars and using that number as a benchmark. As individuals shared their estimates I used a thick, dark marker to record them on sticky notes. I arbitrarily slapped each sticky note on the board before taking the next estimate. (I chose to write the numbers myself in order to save time, but I have also done this activity by giving each student a sticky note and marker and having students record and post their own estimates.)

When we finished recording and posting the estimates, we had a board haphazardly filled with sticky notes. This "mess of numbers" became the source of a rich discussion about data.

"Hmm," I said, "there are a lot of numbers up here. Look at them carefully and see if you can identify the lowest number and the highest number on the board."

I gave the students a few moments to peruse the board and waited until many hands were raised. I called on Kellen, who told us 16 and 210. I checked in with the rest of the students to see if they agreed. After establishing consensus, I pulled the 16 sticky off the board and put it at the far left end. Then I put the 210 sticky at the right side of the board.

"OK," I said, "the rest of your estimates are between sixteen and two hundred ten. That helps us figure out the range. What is the range?"

I saw that some of the students were counting the sticky notes on the board instead of calculating the actual difference between the two numbers, so I clarified my question. "I'm noticing that some of you are trying to figure out how many sticky notes are on the board. You're right that all the sticky notes are between sixteen and two ten, but what you need to figure out is the difference between sixteen and two hundred ten. The sticky notes show some of the numbers, but we need to find out how many there'd be if we had every number between sixteen and two ten." I recorded the range on the board to help students visualize the problem: *16–210*.

This explanation helped the students get on track, but again I noticed that some students were struggling to do the arithmetic mentally. I told the students that they could work on the problem in their math journals if they liked. After a couple of minutes I called for their attention and asked who would like to tell us how he or she found the range. Here was a nice opportunity to have a brief number talk.

"It's one hundred ninety-four," D'andre announced.

The class agreed, so I pushed on.

"How do you know?" I asked.

"Because I just did two ten minus sixteen and that's one ninety-four," he explained.

I knew that D'andre had done the standard subtraction algorithm in his math journal so I didn't pursue it further.

"Did anyone do it a different way?" I asked the class.

"I added up," Marsha announced.

"Tell us how you did that," I encouraged.

"Well, I added four to sixteen to get to twenty. Then I added hundred, so I was at one hundred twenty. Then I added ninety more to get to two hundred ten."

"So how did you know the range was one hundred ninety-four?" I asked.

"Because I added four plus hundred plus ninety, and that's one ninety-four," Marsha explained.

Since Marsha's strategy might not make complete sense to students who had not used it or been exposed to it before, I decided to record it on the board to demonstrate her thinking for other students. I wrote:

$$16 + \underline{4} = 20$$
$$20 + \underline{100} = 120$$
$$120 + \underline{90} = 210$$
$$4 + 100 + 90 = 194$$

"I added and subtracted," Tina shared next.

"How did you do that?" I queried.

Tina explained her method. "Well I started at sixteen and added one hundred. Then I was at one hundred sixteen. I added another one hundred and that made two hundred sixteen. I was past two hundred ten, so had to subtract six."

I realized this method called for a visual model as well. I wrote on the board:

$$16 + \underline{100} = 116$$
$$116 + \underline{100} = 216$$
$$216 - \underline{6} = 210$$
$$100 + 100 = 200, \; 200 - 6 = 194$$

"Great," I said. "There are a lot of different ways to find the range. The range helps you know about the data and which numbers you're dealing with. There are some other things to look at that also help you analyze data and figure out what it all might mean. But as I'm looking at the board, I still see a big mess. Let's try to put the numbers in order. We already have the sixteen at one end and the two hundred ten at the other. Who would like to help arrange the rest of the numbers?"

Many hands flew into the air. I called on Esteban and Paulina to come forward and rearrange the sticky notes. They got a lot of help from the rest of the class. I helped them by asking questions such as, "Which is the next lowest number?" and "Are there any numbers between these two numbers?" I also showed them that when two sticky notes had the same number, they should put one above the other. It took them only about a minute to get the sticky notes in order. Then we had an instant graph and we were ready to look for the median and the mode.

"Now let's find the mode. How can we tell what the mode is?" I asked the class.

"It's the number you see the most," Tina reminded us.

"So what is the mode?" I asked, pointing to the graph. Since the sticky notes were placed along the board in a horizontal line with repeated numbers stacked on top of one another, it was easy to see that 100 was the mode because it had the tallest column.

"Now let's see if we can find the median. How can we do that?" I asked.

"The median is the one in the middle," Chip explained.

"So how can we tell which one is in the middle?" I wondered aloud.

"Count up all the sticky notes and halve that number," Kesha suggested.

"That would work," I agreed.

"Start at each end and move into the middle," Nicole offered.

"Let's try that," I agreed.

I asked for two volunteers to help us. Michael and Tanisa obliged. Michael started at 16 and Tanisa started at 210. They each put a finger on the first sticky note on their end and then walked toward each other as we counted each note. They were nose-to-nose when Michael had a finger on 60 and Tanisa was touching 75.

"Hmm," I observed, "there seem to be two sticky notes in the middle, not just one. I wonder what that's about."

"It's because there's an even number of estimates, " Miguel explained.

"Yes," I agreed. "Does anybody know how to handle it if there are two numbers in the middle instead of just one?"

There were universal looks of uncertainty, so I explained the mathematical convention to the students. "If you have an odd number of data, you can find the one that's exactly in the middle, and that's the median. If you have an even number, you take the two numbers in the middle and find the number that's between those two."

Having told them the convention, I gave the students a few moments to determine that the median was 67.5.

"OK," I said, "let's review what we know about the data." I wrote on the board:

Range: 194
Mode: 100
Median: 67.5

"This kind of information is very useful," I concluded. "When we started we just had a messy bunch of numbers on the board. Now we have some information about the numbers that can help us think about those numbers and see how they fit together. If we wanted to go outside and actually count the cars parked around the school, we could see if the actual number was within the range of our estimates. We could also compare the actual number to the mode and median of our estimates. When you know the range, mode, and median, you can organize and analyze mathematical information."

Extending the Activity

There are many ways to adapt and extend this activity. By asking different questions, you can easily manipulate the magnitude of the numbers and the size of the range. At times you might choose to collect the data and just focus in depth on one aspect. Asking questions such as, "Who would need to know this information?" and "Who would care what the mode is?" requires students to apply theses concepts to real-life examples. As a homework assignment students can look for graphs in newspapers and magazines and bring them in to discuss and analyze.

Looking at Data can also be connected to different math strands. You can adjust your questions to fit your current math focus. When studying measurement, have students estimate things such as paces across the room, square feet of classroom space, or volume of a container. After making their estimates and analyzing the data, they can do the actual measuring. During a probability unit, have students collect data about dice or spinners and analyze the significance of the range, mode, and median in that context.

Number Strings

16

CONTENT AREA

Number and Operations

MATERIALS

■ optional: overhead projector

TIME

five to ten minutes

Overview

In this activity, students practice mentally combining numbers in different ways using number strings. For this lesson, a number string is an expression, written in a horizontal format, that includes more than two addends. It's best to introduce students to *Number Strings* after they have had some experience solving problems with two addends, followed by number talks.

With time and experience, students begin to use their understanding of number relations to solve problems. For example, students might use their knowledge of benchmark numbers (10, 25, 100, 1,000) to recombine numbers and simplify the problem. Another approach used by many students in the intermediate grades is compensation. In the number string $32 + 23 + 51$, a student might take two from the 32 to make it 30 and then give the two to the 23 to make it 25. Number strings also offer the occasion to use mathematical notation, such as parentheses, and discuss its meaning in the context of equations.

Activity Directions

1. Have students brainstorm ways to make one hundred. Write the equations on the board or an overhead.
2. Record a number string on the board for students to solve (e.g., $23 + 14 + 250 + 12 + 50 =$).
3. Allow a minute or so for students to solve the problem mentally.
4. During partner talk, direct the students to talk to a partner about their answer and strategy for solving the number string.
5. During whole-class discussion, elicit answers and strategies from a few volunteers and represent students' strategies numerically on the board.
6. Repeat Steps 2–5 using a new number string.

Key Questions

- What did you do to solve the problem?
- Did anyone solve the problem in a different way?
- Tell us where you started and why.
- Were there any number combinations that made it easier to solve the problem?

From the Classroom

I introduced *Number Strings* to a group of fourth and fifth graders by focusing on one hundred. I chose a familiar benchmark number so students could focus on the mechanics of number strings rather than having to strain over the mental computation.

"We're going to do some math that focuses on one hundred," I told the class, "so before we begin the activity, let's take a few minutes to think about one hundred. What are some ways to make one hundred?"

"Fifty plus fifty," several students responded almost immediately.

I wrote on the board:

$50 + 50 = 100$

Then I called for other combinations. In a short time we had a nice list on the board.

$50 + 50 = 100$
$90 + 10 = 100$
$20 + 80 = 100$
$30 + 70 = 100$
$99 + 1 = 100$
$98 + 2 = 100$
$86 + 14 = 100$
$75 + 25 = 100$

Next I asked the students to think of ways to make 100 using more than two addends. Many of the students used the two-addend equations already on the board and broke the numbers apart further to make three-addend equations. For example, they moved from $50 + 50 = 100$ to $50 + 25 + 25 = 100$. The students quickly generated a list of equations, which I recorded on the board.

"OK," I told the students, "you know a lot of different ways to make one hundred. I'm going to write an expression with three numbers on the board. You are going to find the answer mentally. You might find the job easier if you try to use what you know about one hundred and hunt for hundreds." I wrote on the board:

$$50 + 12 + 50 =$$

I deliberately chose a fairly obvious number string to build students' confidence and to provide scaffolding for more difficult problems. After giving the students a bit of time to solve the problem, I asked them to tell me the answer in unison. The response was unanimous and correct. Now was the time to push the communication.

"Yes," I agreed, "the answer is one hundred twelve. What did you do to solve the problem?"

"First I saw the fifty and fifty and that makes one hundred," Anny explained. "Then I added twelve more to it and got one hundred twelve."

I recorded Anny's idea on the board.

$$50 + 12 + 50 =$$
$$50 + 50 = 100$$
$$100 + 12 = 112$$

"Did anyone solve it a different way?" I asked.

Most students had seen the one hundred first and then added twelve, so I moved on to the next number string.

$$60 + 21 + 40 =$$

Here again students had little problem finding the sum. Several students explained that they had added the sixty and forty first and then added twenty-one to the one hundred. I decided to offer a less obvious number string to see how the students would approach it. I was especially interested to see if they would continue to hunt for hundreds or find other ways to deal with the problem. I wrote the third number string on the board.

$$76 + 24 + 51 =$$

Knowing that this number string was more challenging, I gave the students more time to think about it before eliciting responses. I wanted to make sure they had enough to time to feel confident in their mental computation. I also wanted to give them time to notice their own thinking so that they would be better prepared to talk to the class about it. I modeled this by looking at the problem and appearing to solve it mentally myself.

I had the students respond in unison when I asked for the sum. They had the correct answer.

"Great," I told them. "Now, who's willing to tell us where you started when you first approached the problem?"

Many students raised their hands. I called on Howard.

"First I did six and four make ten," he began.

"Where did the six and four come from and why did you start there?" I probed.

"Oh," Howard replied, "I took the six from the seventy-six and the four from the twenty-four. I started there because it's easy to work with tens. Also, it turned the seventy-six and twenty-four into easy tens, too. Then I did seventy and twenty equals ninety. Ten and ninety make one hundred, and then I added fifty-one to it to get one hundred fifty-one."

I recorded Howard's explanation on the board.

Howard's Way

$$6 + 4 = 10$$
$$70 + 20 = 90$$
$$90 + 10 = 100$$
$$100 + 51 = 151$$

"Did anyone find other ways to get easy number combinations?" I asked.

Several students raised their hands. I called on Katrina.

"I borrowed one from the seventy-six and gave it to the twenty-four," Katrina began.

"Why did you decide to do that?" I inquired.

"Because then it's easier and I could make one hundred," she explained. "I turned it into seventy-five plus twenty-five, and that's an easy one. It's even on the board already. Then I just added the fifty-one and I got one hundred fifty-one."

Katrina was referring to our initial discussion about ways to make one hundred. I had left the equations on the board and I was pleased to hear the list was useful. I recorded Katrina's strategy on the board next to Howard's.

Katrina's Way

$$76 - 1 = 75$$
$$24 + 1 = 25$$
$$75 + 25 = 100$$
$$100 + 51 = 151$$

I had a few more students share their thinking about the number string. Several students started with the ones and then proceeded to the tens. A few students added all the tens first and then went back to deal with the ones.

I felt this was a fine introduction to *Number Strings*. Students had a variety of ways to solve the equations. Furthermore, they were willing to share their thinking and listen to each other's ideas. I knew that as the year progressed I would be able to employ *Number Strings* as a way to give students practice with mental computation and to focus on specific arithmetic topics we were studying.

Extending the Activity

Different number strings can be used in the classroom as the year progresses. For instance, if the goal is for students to practice finding combinations of one hundred or one thousand, number strings like these could be useful:

$$25 + 17 + 75 = \qquad 32 + 44 + 68 = \qquad 300 + 400 + 700 =$$

Number Strings also works well with multiplication and when introducing and extending work with fractions and decimals. Number strings provide students valuable practice with mental computation and combining numbers in efficient ways.

When teaching *Number Strings*, encourage the students to look at the whole problem to see if they can find benchmark numbers or use familiar combinations. This habit will greatly improve their facility with all types of arithmetic.

17

Odd Number Wins

CONTENT AREA

Number and
Operations

MATERIALS

- counters, cubes, or
  tiles, 15 per pair of
  students
- overhead projector

TIME

ten to fifteen minutes

Overview

In this logic game, students explore number combinations and patterns and their effect on the results of simple addition problems. As partners take turns removing counters from a common pile, they use logical thinking to consider their total, their partner's total, and the amount left in the pile. While the mechanics of the game are fairly simple, the logical thinking required to develop winning strategies pushes students' mathematical reasoning. Discussing experiences with the whole class brings the logic and language to the surface of the activity.

Activity Directions

1. Start by placing fifteen counters on the overhead projector.
2. Invite a student to join you in modeling a game in front of the class.
3. Explain the rules of the game:
   - Players can take one, two, or three counters on his or her turn.
   - Players continue taking turns until all the counters are gone.
   - The player with the odd number of counters at the end is the winner.
4. Lead a brief discussion with students to determine some mathematical rules that might help them as they play the game:
   - odd + odd = even
   - even + even = even
   - odd + even = odd
5. Play one round of the game with the student volunteer.
6. Write on the board focus questions for students to consider as they play the game in pairs.
   - *Does it matter who goes first?*
   - *What strategies did you use?*

7. Let students play with partners at their tables.
8. After students play several rounds of the game, lead a class discussion based on the focus questions.

Key Questions

- Does it matter who goes first?
- What strategies did you use?

From the Classroom

I started at the overhead projector to model a game of *Odd Number Wins* in front of a class of fifth graders. I placed fifteen counters on the overhead and I invited Miguel to join me.

"So here's the deal," I explained to the class. "We've got fifteen chips on the overhead. Miguel and I are going to take turns pulling some chips. On each turn we can take one, two, or three chips. After we've taken all the chips, we will check to see how many we have. How can we tell who won?"

"Whoever has the most!" Danelle responded.

"Aha," I said, "that's the way to find the winner in most games, but this game is a little different. You win if you end up with an odd number of chips. It doesn't matter who has the most, it only matters who has an odd amount."

"I wonder if we can find any mathematical rules that apply to this type of situation," I said to the class. "What happens when you add an odd number plus an odd number?"

We had a brief discussion and generated some examples of various simple addition scenarios. We concluded the following:

$$odd + odd\ = even$$
$$even + even = even$$
$$odd + even\ = odd$$

I felt it was useful to spend a few minutes making these ideas explicit. These concepts might serve as a reference point for students while playing the game. They also invite further investigation as an extension to the activity.

"Let's start a game," I said to Miguel. "Do you want to go first or should I go first?"

"You can go first," Miguel acquiesced.

"OK," I began, "I'll take two. Am I allowed to do that?"

"Yes," the class responded.

Miguel then took three. After each turn I checked with the whole class to make sure we were following the rules and to ask how many counters were left and how many each of us had. This questioning kept the whole class involved even though only two of us were playing. After we completed the game I gave the class some final instructions.

"In a minute or so you are going to go back to your tables and play *Odd Number Wins* with a partner," I explained. "The first few times you play, you will just be getting to know how the game works. But after a few games you'll be able to concentrate on the mathematics. There are two questions we'll focus on when we get back together to discuss your experiences." I wrote on the board:

Does it matter who goes first?
What strategies did you use?

I sent the students off to their tables to play the game in pairs. The students were very engaged, although some were overly invested in winning. I reminded the class that winning was not the goal of the game. The goal was to have some mathematical ideas to discuss when we talked about the questions on the board. I gave the students enough time to play several games. Then I called the students back together so we could discuss their discoveries.

"So now you've got some experience with *Odd Number Wins*," I told the students. "Let's think about these questions. Does it matter who goes first?"

The class was split on this question. Many students were convinced it made no difference, while others had strategies that required either they or their opponents went first. I decided to let this controversy simmer. We were not going to come to consensus in a brief period, and as winning strategies emerged over time, students would see more clearly whether who went first mattered. I recorded both possibilities on the list of strategies.

"Let's talk about other strategies," I suggested. "What types of things were you doing that helped you end up with an odd number or helped your partner end up with an even number?"

As students shared their strategies I recorded them on the board. In a short time we had a nice list:

Go first.
Let your partner go first.

Pay attention to your partner's total.
Take odd numbers.
Take one or three, then take two, then take one or three.
Pick odd, even, odd, even . . .
Start with an even number.
Have an odd number and leave one for your partner.
Pick three every turn and take whatever is left at the end.
Pay attention to how many are left.

"Wow," I remarked, "you got a lot of ideas after playing only a short time. I'm going to leave these strategies on the board, and the next time you play *Odd Number Wins* you can test out some of the strategies. You'll probably find that some of the strategies work sometimes and some of them work all of the time. When you find some that work all of the time, the next mathematical question for you to think about is why that strategy works. Also, you might develop more strategies as you play more. You can add those to the list we started."

I thanked the students for their work and thinking and told them I was looking forward to hearing about the discoveries they would make as they continued to play *Odd Number Wins*.

Extending the Activity

Language plays a key role in *Odd Number Wins*. In addition to conducting oral discussions about strategies, have students incorporate writing. Use the key questions as writing prompts and have students reflect in their math journals. As students play over time, they will begin to develop winning strategies. Push the students to explain the logic of the strategies and their connections to odd and even numbers in order to make the game a rich mathematical experience worth revisiting over time.

Once students develop winning strategies that they can explain, challenge them further by slightly altering the game. Have students start with twenty-one counters instead of fifteen. Or change the amount of counters they're allowed to take on each turn.

Another extension involves exploring odd and even addends in more depth. Use a T-chart to systematically consider all the two-addend combinations of fifteen possible in the game.

Player A	Player B
1	14
2	13
3	12
4	11
5	10
6	9
7	8
8	7
9	6
10	5
11	4
12	3
13	2
14	1

I used the list of combinations to open a discussion about whether or not it was possible for both players to end up with an odd number of chips. The T-chart provided a visual model and we hypothesized that when an odd number is broken down into two addends, one of the addends will be odd and the other will be even. Students also noticed the alternating odd-even patterns in the two columns. While a discussion about the nature of odd and even numbers is not the focus of the activity, follow-up sessions can take advantage of an opportunity to expose students to some number theory and prepare them for future explorations.

Over or Under

18

Overview

Over or Under is a quick estimation activity that helps students quantify objects and situations in their immediate surroundings. Students focus on benchmark numbers in order to estimate amounts of different items in their classroom. Easy to implement and engaging for students, this activity turns even a few minutes into a rich mathematical experience.

Activity Directions

1. Ask students to generate a list of items in the classroom that could be counted.
2. Record their ideas on the board or on overhead.
3. Write some benchmark numbers on the board (e.g., *10, 25, 50, 75, 100, 250, 500, 750, 1,000*) and review the concept of benchmark numbers with the class.
4. Pick an item from the student-generated list.
5. Ask students if they think the actual number of items is over or under each of the benchmark numbers on the board.
6. Have students share their thinking.
7. Repeat Steps 5 and 6 using a different item from the list.

Key Questions

- What are benchmark numbers?
- Is your estimate over or under ___?
- How much over or under is your estimate?

CONTENT AREA

Number and Operations

Measurement

MATERIALS

■ optional: overhead projector

TIME

five to ten minutes

From the Classroom

Robin Gordon asked her fourth graders to look around the room and talk to a partner about things that they could count. After a few moments students shared their ideas as she listed them on the board.

names on Popsicle sticks
hearts on the calendar
posters
books
numbers on the number line
letters in the alphabet
word study words
molecules
tables
chairs
watches
stars on the flag
boxes
pencils
paper
rectangles in the shelves

"There's a lot of stuff to count in this room," Robin remarked. "Now I'm going to write some benchmark numbers on the board. As I write these numbers, think about why they're called benchmarks. Just what are benchmark numbers?" Robin used another part of the board to write a list of numbers.

10
25
50
75
100
250
500
750
1,000

"Those are the easy numbers," Ricky responded.
"Like you use them for money," Betty added.
"They're numbers you use for rounding," Ontario explained.

"Those are all good ways to talk about benchmark numbers," the teacher agreed. "These benchmark numbers are friendly numbers that we're familiar with, and they're easy to use and compute with."

Next Robin wrote on the board:

Over or Under

"What we're going to do now is use these two lists. We've got a list of things to count and we've got a list of benchmark numbers. I'm going to pick something from your list and you're going to estimate whether the actual amount is over or under these benchmark numbers. Let's start with the first item—names on Popsicle sticks."

Robin had a cup with Popsicle sticks in the front of the room. Each stick had one student's name on it. Robin used these sticks to randomly call on students or to pick a student for a special task. She chose to focus first on the Popsicle sticks because it would be fairly easy for students to know the amount.

She picked up the cup and pointed to the number 10 on the board. "So what do you think?" she asked the class. "Is the number of names on these sticks over or under ten?"

"Over!" was the overwhelming response from the class.

"Is it over or under twenty-five?" Robin asked, moving to the next benchmark number on the board.

This time there was a mixed chorus of "overs" and "unders."

"Hmm," Robin said, "we've reached the point where people have different ideas about this question. Let's talk about it."

"Well," Raquel explained, "I think it's under because we only have twenty-one students in the class."

"Yeah, but we each have more than one name," Mitchell countered.

Robin pulled one of the sticks out of the cup. She confirmed that it had a first name and a last name on it.

"Oh," Robin said, "this makes it trickier. I need to clarify the question. How many names are on each stick?"

"Two," the class responded.

"OK," she continued, "so we'll count all the first names and last names on the sticks. Now talk to a partner about whether you think the number of names is over or under twenty-five."

Robin gave the students a few moments to discuss this and do some mental computation. Most of them agreed that there were forty-two names. Robin continued the questioning.

"So what's the consensus?" she asked. "Is it over or under twenty-five?"

"Over!" the class replied in unison.

"Moving on to the next benchmark number," Robin continued, "is it over or under fifty?"

The class replied, "Under!"

"Can anyone explain how you know it's under fifty?" Robin asked.

"Because there are twenty-one kids in the class and each kid has a first and last name," Herman explained. "If you double twenty-one you get forty-two, and that's less than fifty."

"Makes sense to me," Robin agreed. "Let's check that to make sure. There are two names on each Popsicle stick, so count by twos as I pull each stick out of the can."

The students counted by twos as Robin removed the sticks one by one. They ended at 42, confirming their idea. Robin then had them talk to a partner about how much the actual total was over and under the two nearest benchmarks. The students concluded that 42 was 17 more than 25 and 18 less than 50.

"This time let's think about the number of pencils in the room. Talk to a partner about your estimates and then we'll use the benchmark numbers to find out about your ideas."

While the students talked, Robin wrote a sentence frame on the board:

The number of pencils in the room is over/under ___.

She called the class to order and explained, "Sometimes it's confusing to just give a one-word answer, so I wrote a sentence up here to help us keep track of what we're talking about."

Robin referred back to the benchmark numbers. She started with ten and the students all agreed the number of pencils was over ten. Similarly, they agreed the number was over twenty-five. When they got to fifty there was a mix of responses. Robin knew this was the place to stop and have a conversation.

"Some of you think the number of pencils in the room is over fifty and some of you think it's under. Let's hear some of your thinking on this."

"I think it's over fifty," Tula said. "Everyone has about two pencils and there are also pencils at the supply table."

"Also, Ms. Gordon has some pencils," Brandy added.

"And Mrs. A. gave us each a pencil for Valentine's Day," William said.

"But some people took those home," Jesse countered.

"And maybe some got lost," furthered Khalil.

"A lot of factors to consider," Robin validated. "Show me with your thumbs what you're thinking now. Put your thumb up if you think there are over fifty pencils in the class. Put your thumb down if you think we have under fifty pencils."

Robin decided to have students use their thumbs so that she could see each individual's response. This participation structure also gives a more quiet way for the whole class to respond at once. Most of the students had their thumbs up, so Robin asked them to talk to a small group about whether they thought there were over seventy-five or under seventy-five pencils in the class. This led to another lively exchange. Students used a combination of data gathering, mental computation, and classroom lore to justify their estimates. Robin knew that these types of discussions would continue in future episodes of *Over or Under*.

Extending the Activity

Use whole number benchmarks to introduce *Over or Under* to the class. Fractions, decimals, and percents work well once students understand the structure of the activity. The benchmarks might be $\frac{1}{4}$, $\frac{1}{2}$, and $\frac{3}{4}$ or .25, .5, and .75 or 25 percent, 50 percent, and 75 percent. To generate a list that works well for fractions, ask students to think of things in the room that are parts of groups (e.g., people with short-sleeve shirts, fiction books in the class library) or ratios (e.g., boys to girls, pens to pencils).

Some students will be very interested in finding the actual number of the items discussed. Depending on the item, this counting can be done as part of the activity or student volunteers can count at a later point and report back to the class. Once the actual number is known, students can do mental computation to find the closest benchmark number. They can also calculate how much over or under the actual number is from a particular benchmark.

Over or Under also works well for measurement. Have students estimate the length, width, height, weight, or capacity of things in the room in relation to benchmark numbers.

19

Personal Numbers

CONTENT AREA

Number and
Operations

MATERIALS

- optional: overhead
  projector

TIME

ten to fifteen minutes

Overview

Personal Numbers is a fun way for students to get to know each other and
think about ways numbers are integrated into their lives. In this activity
students explore the role numbers play in their lives outside the classroom.
Often students feel alienated or intimidated by numbers because numbers
are not as obvious in their world as printed text is. *Personal Numbers* begins to open students up to the realization that numbers are all around
them and serve a variety of purposes in their lives. Not only do numbers
represent quantities, but they also function as descriptors, markers for
comparison, milestones, locations, and labels. *Personal Numbers* helps
students generate examples of these uses and become aware of the function of numbers outside of math class.

Activity Directions

1. Share some personal numbers and tell students you're going to ask
   them to guess what the numbers might represent.
2. Lead a brief discussion focusing on what is reasonable and what isn't
   reasonable in regard to the numbers.
3. Have students talk in small groups about what each of your personal
   numbers could reasonably represent.
4. Have students share their guesses about what each of your personal
   numbers represents. Ask students to explain why their guesses are
   reasonable.
5. Reveal what each of your personal numbers represents.
6. Introduce to students nominal, ordinal, and cardinal numbers.
   Explain the purpose of each type of number and point out examples
   of each in your list of personal numbers.
7. Ask students to brainstorm their own personal numbers, write them
   down, and next to each, note what the number represents.

8. Let individuals share their personal numbers, and have classmates try to guess the significance of each number.

Key Questions

- Is that a reasonable guess? Explain.
- What might that number mean?
- What couldn't that number stand for?

From the Classroom

"We've been working together for a while now," I told Robin Gordon's fourth graders. "You probably know some things about me from our time together. There are other things you can tell about me just by looking at me. I'm going to open up today and share even more about myself. I'm going to share my personal numbers."

"Huh?" Eddie blurted.

"Everyone has personal numbers. They are numbers that are special to you because they represent something important in your life. I'm going to show you some of my personal numbers and give you some time to think about what they might mean to me." I wrote on the board:

$3805\frac{1}{2}$
1962
7.5
2001
19
2
46
4
8
$63\frac{1}{2}$

"Before you start guessing what these personal numbers are about, you need to know what we're focusing on. We're going to pay attention to what's reasonable and what's unreasonable," I explained. I wrote *reasonable* and *unreasonable* on the board.

"When you look at my numbers, what would be a reasonable possibility for one of them?"

"Maybe you were born in nineteen sixty-two," Angel suggested.

"Is that reasonable? How old would I be if I were born in nineteen sixty-two? Talk to a partner about that."

I gave the students a few moments to discuss and do the mental computation. Then I modeled how they could figure it out by jumping up by decades.

"What's nineteen sixty-two plus ten years?" I asked, holding up one finger.

"Nineteen seventy-two," the class responded.

"Plus ten more years?" I asked, while holding up another finger.

"Nineteen eighty-two."

"Plus ten more?" I asked.

"Nineteen ninety-two."

"Plus ten more?"

The students replied, "two thousand two."

"OK," I said, looking at the four fingers I was holding up, "that's ten, twenty, thirty, forty years to get to two thousand two. But it's two thousand five, so we need to add three more years since I already had my birthday this year."

"That's forty-three," Mitchell declared.

"So is that reasonable?" I refocused. "Could I have been born in nineteen sixty-two?"

"Yes," the class concurred.

"Give me another example of a reasonable guess," I requested.

"Nineteen, two, four, and eight could be the ages of your kids," Tula noted.

"Is that reasonable?" I asked. "Could I have kids those ages?"

"Sure," Ricky replied for the class.

"OK, so those are good examples of reasonable guesses. Can someone give an example of an unreasonable guess?"

"It's unreasonable that you learned to walk when you were nineteen years old," Raquel offered.

"Yes," I agreed. "That would make me a very late bloomer."

"It's unreasonable that you have forty-six kids," Khalil shared.

"Very unreasonable," I agreed. "So I think you're getting it. You're going to have a few minutes to talk about my personal numbers. Your goal is to try to think of reasonable meanings for all of these numbers. It doesn't matter whether you actually guess the correct answer. The important part is the reasonableness. I'll tell you what all these numbers stand for later so you don't have to worry about getting them right."

I let the students talk in small groups about my personal numbers. Their discussions were animated and their ideas very creative. After a few minutes I called them back together to hear some of their ideas.

"It's reasonable that you have two sisters," Brandy began.

"It's reasonable that your son is eight years old," William contributed.

"Well, seven point five is the same as seven and a half," Mitchell began. "And seven and a half could be your shoe size, so seven point five could be your shoe size."

"Is that reasonable?" I asked the class.

"Yes," the students agreed and began to discuss their own shoe sizes.

I asked for their attention back and got them ready for the next part of the activity. I wrote the actual meaning of each number on the board, then I referred them to the list.

$3805\frac{1}{2}$	*house #*
1962	*birth year*
7.5	*shoe size*
2001	*car year*
19	*years teaching*
2	*son's grade*
46	*states visited*
4	*TVs in house*
8	*son's age*
$63\frac{1}{2}$	*height in inches*

"So now you know where my personal numbers come from and what they mean," I said to the class. "Now it's your turn to think about some of your own personal numbers. Before you do that, however, I want to point out something to you. Numbers are used for different purposes. For example, three eight zero five and a half is more like a name. It's a number used to identify my house. Those kinds of numbers are called *nominal* numbers. If you think about sports uniforms, they usually have numbers on them. Those are nominal numbers, too. They're a way to help identify or give a name to the player." I wrote *nominal—name* next to $3805\frac{1}{2}$ on the board.

"There are two other kinds of numbers I'm going to tell you about. My son's grade is an *ordinal* number. He's in second grade and that tells the order of the grade he's in. First, second, third, fourth—those are ordinal numbers." I wrote *ordinal—order* on the board next to 2.

"Finally, there are the numbers we use when we're counting to find out how many. Those are called *cardinal* numbers. I've been teaching for nineteen years. The nineteen tells how many years, so it's a cardinal number."

I wrote *cardinal—how many* on the board next to 19.

"So now it's your turn to write down some of your personal numbers. Try to write at least ten. Also, see if you can think of some nominal, ordinal, and cardinal numbers to use. You can use some of my ideas from the board to help you get started. But some of my personal number ideas won't work for you since you're not adults with kids and jobs and cars yet."

I solicited suggestions from the students for other personal numbers they might come up with. Suggestions ranged from number of siblings to countries visited to highest score on a video game. When I was satisfied that the students had enough ideas, I sent them back to their seats to begin writing down their own personal numbers. I encouraged them to write the number and then write what it represented right next to it. Ironically, it's easy to forget what your own personal numbers stand for sometimes. I planned to have different students share a few of their personal numbers with the class on my next visit. The rest of the class would try to come up with reasonable guesses about the numbers shared.

Extending the Activity

There are many versions of *Personal Numbers*. In order to incorporate more writing into the activity, have students write clues for their personal numbers and read them to the class. If the class is studying a particular area of math (e.g., fractions, decimals, percents), teachers can request that students incorporate those types of numbers into their lists. Modeling and brainstorming might be necessary to help students think of categories for personal numbers and ways to express the numbers. For example, teachers might need to help students see that the same idea can be represented by different types of numbers. A student might say she has three girls in her family of five children. The teacher can help the student see that she can also express that fact as a fraction—three-fifths of the children in her family are girls.

Race for Twenty

20

Overview

Race for Twenty is a counting game in which partners employ strategic and logical thinking. While the game itself is quite simple, the mathematics embedded within it makes it an exciting activity for upper-elementary students. The teacher plays a crucial role in bringing the mathematics to the surface of the game. Discussion questions lead the students to become aware of their strategies and the structure of the logic inherent in the game. Discussions about the game are far more important than the game itself. The real learning happens as students listen to each other's ideas and analyze strategic thinking. *Race for Twenty* is from the nim family of logic games. There are many other nim games that students enjoy. When students experience other nim games (see "Odd Number Wins"), they can compare them and begin to understand the logical structure of the game strategies.

Activity Directions

1. Have students pair up.
2. Tell students that they are going to play a counting game. The goal is to be the person who says "twenty."
3. Explain the rules to the class: On each turn, a student may count aloud either one or two numbers (e.g., Player A: 1, 2; Player B: 3; Player A: 4; Player B: 5, 6; etc.). Play continues until one player reaches 20.
4. Model a game with a student partner.
5. Write focus points on the board, explaining to students that there will be a discussion based on the points:
   • what you noticed
   • your strategies
6. Let students play several times.

CONTENT AREA

Algebra

MATERIALS

■ optional: overhead projector

TIME

five to ten minutes

7. Lead a discussion about the game based on the focus points listed on the board. Record students' ideas on the board or an overhead.
8. Have partners choose a strategy they hadn't thought of before and test it out as they play the game a few more times.
9. Lead a brief discussion to find out which ideas seem to work all of the time and which seem to work only some of the time.

Key Questions

- What did you notice after you played a few times?
- What strategy did you use to try to get to twenty?
- Does it matter who goes first?

From the Classroom

Tina Rasori's third and fourth graders were eager to learn a new game. After having the students pair up, I quickly went over the ground rules so we could jump right in.

"So this game is called *Race for Twenty*," I explained to the class. "It's a counting game you play with a partner. When it's your turn, you can count one or two numbers. Your partner counts on one or two numbers from where you left off. Whoever says 'twenty' is the winner. I'm going to play one game in front of the whole class with a partner. That way you can see how the game goes and ask any questions. Who would like to come up here and be my partner?"

Many students raised their hands. I chose Antoinette.

"Do you want to go first or should I?" I asked Antoinette.

"You can," she said.

"Let's see," I began, "one, two."

"Three, four," Antoinette responded.

"Five," I said.

"Six, seven," Antoinette continued.

I stopped there to check in with the class. While this was a two-person activity, I wanted to make sure the whole class felt responsible for paying attention and making sure we were following the rules.

"Is she allowed to do that?" I asked.

"Yes," was the somewhat indignant response from the majority. The students wanted the game to continue.

"OK," I said. "Eight, nine."

"Ten, eleven," Antoinette said.

"Twelve," I countered.

"Thirteen, fourteen," Antoinette continued.

I hesitated there and closed my eyes for a few seconds. Then I scratched my head and stroked my chin. I wanted to explicitly model for the class that this game involved more than just rote counting. I wanted to the students to actually see that I was thinking before taking my next turn.

"Fifteen," I finally said with authority.

"Sixteen, seventeen," Antoinette responded.

Again I slowed the pace and modeled some thinking time. This time also allowed the students to catch on to my dilemma. A murmur of excitement pulsed through the class as the students realized the teacher was about to lose.

"Uh oh," I said. "I think I'm in trouble. Eighteen?"

"Nineteen, twenty," Antoinette announced in triumph as the students applauded.

I was glad to serve as the foil in this introductory game. My relatively painless loss showed students that the competitive aspect of the game was less important than the game itself and the thinking it involved. I made a point of mentioning this to the students before I sent them off to play *Race for Twenty* with a partner.

"So now you've seen how to play the game and you know it's about thinking, not about winning or losing," I summarized. "You next job is to play with a partner. But when you're playing, you'll actually have two jobs. First, you'll be getting practice and learning how the game works. Second, you'll be thinking about a couple of things." I went to the board and wrote:

What You Noticed
Your Strategies

I left enough room between the two so that I could fill in some student comments later. It was important for me to preview the points that I planned to use for discussion later. This way, students knew they were accountable for more than just rotely playing the game. Also, they got some time to prepare for the discussion in advance so it was less likely that my summarizing questions would be met with blank stares. I gave the students a few minutes to play the game with their partners. Then I called them back together to summarize the experience. Several students were eager to share, so I soon had some interesting ideas written on the board.

What You Noticed

Adelai: If your partner says "seventeen, eighteen," you'll win.
Delila: The person who goes first ends up saying "twenty."
Javote: If your partner says "eighteen, nineteen," you'll win.

Jorge: Whoever says "fifteen" loses.
Randall: The person who says two numbers loses.

Your Strategies

Randall: Think before you say a number.
Ani: Make your partner go first.

I looked at all of the ideas on the board. I read each one aloud to make sure all students had access to them. I used these ideas to send the students back to take a deeper look at the game.

"Goodness," I expressed with amazement, "you played for only a few minutes and look at all the ideas you came up with. I am very impressed."

"Now here's your job for the last few minutes. You and your partner are going to pick one of the ideas from up here and test it out. Find something that's interesting or that you hadn't thought of yourself and then play *Race for Twenty* and see if it works."

The children went back to playing *Race for Twenty*. Again, they had a particular focus so that thinking was integrated into game playing. We closed with a brief discussion about their findings. Students discovered that some of the ideas seemed to work all of the time, but others worked only sometimes. I stopped the discussion at that point, knowing that the class would revisit *Race for Twenty*. Further discussions would allow students to investigate which strategies worked consistently. From there, the teacher could begin to push students to understand and explain why the strategies worked. Clearly, *Race for Twenty* is a simple game on the surface, but it provides rich opportunities for mathematical discussions.

Extending the Activity

As students gain experience with *Race for Twenty*, they begin to make discoveries and develop strategies. Many of these early discoveries center around numbers that are good or bad to land on. Sorting these numbers can help students see patterns and begin to devise winning strategies.

If the class has come to a consensus on a winning strategy, create a new challenge by slightly changing the game. For example, you could change the target number from twenty to thirty. Or you could flip the game so that the goal is to make your partner say twenty rather than to be the one to say twenty.

Target 100/Target 0

21

Overview

In this game students apply their understanding of place value in order to make strategic decisions. Students also practice mental addition and subtraction as they determine how close they are to the target number.

Activity Directions

1. Draw six boxes on the board or an overhead.
2. Introduce the game by playing the addition version—*Target 100*. Explain to students that the goal of *Target 100* is to get as close as possible to one hundred without going over by adding up six rolls of the die. Explain that they must use all six rolls of the die, and for each roll, they can make the number a one or a ten.
3. Roll the die and announce the number.
4. Let students decide whether to make the number a ten or a one, and record their number in the first box.
5. Repeat five more times, stopping periodically to let students discuss their current total and what roll they would like to get next.
6. Ask students to find the sum of their six numbers.
7. Ask students to calculate how close they are to one hundred. Have a few students show their computation strategies.
8. Reverse the game by having students start with one hundred and subtract six rolls of the die to get as close to zero as possible without going below.

Key Questions

- What roll would you like to get next? Why?
- How close were you to the target? How do you know?

CONTENT AREA

Number and Operations

MATERIALS

- 1 die
- optional: overhead projector

TIME

ten minutes

From the Classroom

Danielle Pickett's third graders were working on subtraction. I decided to introduce a game that would help them both with the concept of subtraction and subtraction computation. *Target 0* gives students practice with making decisions, estimating, and doing mental computation. Since I wasn't sure how much subtraction the students had done, I decided to introduce the game using an addition version. This way the students could learn the mechanics of the game without getting distracted by difficult computation. Once they understood the workings of the game, I'd move them to the subtraction version.

"I brought one die with me today," I told the class. "That's pretty much all we need for a game called *Target Zero*."

"I know this game," Johannes announced.

"That's great," I responded. "Let's make sure everyone knows how it works."

I drew six boxes in a row on the board.

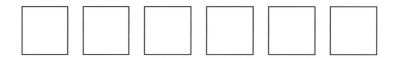

"For a warm-up we're going to play *Target One Hundred* with the whole class," I explained to the students. "I'm going to roll the die and tell you what I got. Then you are going to decide if you want to make that number a ten or a one. For example, if I roll a five, what are your choices?"

"It could be five or fifty," Dylan replied.

"Right," I agreed. "When you decide which number you want, I'll write it in the first box. Then I'll roll again and you'll have the same decision. We'll put that number in the next box. Are there any questions?"

"Are we going to add the numbers up?" Claire asked.

"Yes," I responded.

"What are we trying to get to?" Rebecca asked.

"Good question," I replied. "You're trying to get to one hundred. You might not get exactly one hundred, but you want to get as close as possible. Also, you don't want to go over one hundred. Get it?"

The students nodded.

"One more thing," I added. "Since I drew six boxes on the board, you have to use six rolls. This makes it more challenging. Can you see why?"

"Because we might get fifty and fifty and already be at one hundred," Leah explained.

"Yes," I said, "you need to make sure you spread the numbers out so you don't end up going over one hundred. Are you ready?"

The students nodded their heads, so I rolled the die.

"It's a four," I announced. "Raise your hand if you have an idea about what to do with the four."

"Let's make it forty," Tristan suggested.

I wrote *40* in the first box and rolled again. Soon the board looked like this.

"What's our total now?" I asked the class. I gave the students a minute to compute mentally and then called on Alexa.

"It's seventy-three," Alexa told us.

"Hmm," I said, "you've got a total of seventy-three. I wonder what roll you'd like to get next. Turn to a partner and talk about what would be the best roll and why. Also talk about what you might do with a roll that's not the one you wanted."

I gave the students a few minutes to talk to each other. After some animated discussion, they were ready to share.

"The best roll would be a two," Luke explained. "Because we could make it a twenty and that would give us ninety-three. That's really close to one hundred."

"A three would be too much," Jana chimed in, "because that would make it one hundred three."

I rolled the die and got a 4. The students moaned in disappointment.

"Hold on," I said. "The game's not over. You want to get as close to one hundred as you can without going over. So what do you need to do with the four? Do you want to make it four or forty?"

"We have to make it four because forty is too much. We'll go over one hundred," Otto noted.

I wrote *4* in the last box and asked the students for the total. After the students established that the total was seventy-seven, I decided to take a quick opportunity for them to do some mental computation and hopefully apply some of the strategies they'd learned.

"Well," I said to the class, "your total is seventy-seven. How close to one hundred is seventy-seven?"

"Not that close," Claire commented.

"I think you did pretty well for your first time ever playing *Target One Hundred*," I countered. "But how could you figure out the difference between seventy-seven and one hundred? Talk to a partner and then we'll listen to some of your ideas."

Volunteers shared several different strategies—counting up, subtracting, and rounding to seventy-five, subtracting, and taking away two from the answer. I told them I was sure they would have other opportunities to play *Target 100*.

"Now you're ready for the next level," I told the class. "This time instead of *Target One Hundred*, we're going to play *Target Zero*. Instead of starting with no points and working up to one hundred, you're going to start with one hundred points and try to get down to zero." I wrote on the board:

$$100 - \Box = \bigcirc$$

"The rest of the rules are the same. You need to use six rolls and you decide each time whether to make it a ten or a one. But you're subtracting from one hundred instead of adding up to one hundred."

I rolled the die. It was a 6.

"Let's make it a sixty," Jana suggested.

"What is one hundred minus sixty?" I asked the class.

The students were quick to respond.

I wrote on the board:

$$100 - 60 = 40$$

I rolled several more times, each time asking a volunteer to tell me whether to multiply the roll by one or by ten. In a few minutes the board looked like this:

$$100 - 60 = 40$$
$$40 - 4 = 36$$
$$36 - 6 = 30$$
$$30 - 20 = 10$$

"Hmm," I said, "you've got two more rolls and you want to get to zero. What two rolls would like to get? Talk to a partner about some possibilities."

The students brainstormed many combinations of ten. It's always nice to take advantage of opportunities for students to review their single-digit facts, especially those involving benchmark numbers. This task was a bit tricky because while there are eleven different two-addend possibilities for making ten, most of them are not possible when rolling a die twice. I recorded the possible roll combinations on the board.

6 + 4 = 10
5 + 5 = 10
4 + 6 = 10

"OK," I continued, "let's roll and see what happens."

I ended up rolling a 5 and then another 5, which thrilled the students because they landed exactly at zero. While acknowledging that they would not always be this lucky, the students agreed that *Target 0* was a fun and exciting game.

Extending the Activity

Target 100 and *Target 0* offer a lot of flexibility. Change the target number and/or change the number of rolls required to reach the target. After the games have been modeled with the whole class, students can play on their own in pairs.

22

CONTENT AREA

Number and
Operations

MATERIALS

- optional: overhead
  projector

TIME

five to ten minutes

Tell Me All You Can

Overview

Tell Me All You Can encourages students to think and communicate about equations before actually solving them. Students use what they know about numbers and operations to make statements about an arithmetic problem. In addition to developing number sense, this activity promotes efficient test-taking skills by having students consider the reasonableness and likelihood of different solutions.

Activity Directions

1. Put an open equation on the board or an overhead (e.g., *100 − 67 =*).
2. Ask students to tell you what they know about the problem (not what the answer is). Offer students support using prompts like the following:
   - Is the answer going to be more than or less than one hundred? How do you know?
   - Is the answer going to be more than or less than fifty? How do you know?
   - Make up a story that goes with the problem.
3. Have students prove their conjectures with mathematical explanations.
4. Continue to generate different ideas from the students.
5. Have students solve the problem and explain their strategies.

Key Questions

- What do you know about this problem?
- How do you know?
- Can you tell a story that goes with this problem?

From the Classroom

Lisa Kimbrell's third graders were having some trouble with multidigit subtraction. While they had been exposed to several approaches to solving these problems, they often solved the problems rotely and didn't seem bothered by unreasonable answers. For example, they were unperturbed when the difference was greater than either of the original numbers. They were particularly confused by numbers with zeros in them. They had learned some rules for borrowing and regrouping, but they weren't clear on what to do with the zeros. We decided to try *Tell Me All You Can* as a diagnostic tool and to support their efficiency and accuracy.

"Here's what we're going to try," I told the class. "I'm going to write a subtraction problem on the board. But instead of solving the problem and telling me the answer, you're going to think about this problem in a different way. You're going to tell me everything you know about the problem before you even find the answer. This activity is called *Tell Me All You Can*."

I wrote an equation on the board horizontally.

$$100 - 67 =$$

The horizontal format helps immensely in encouraging students to look at the whole problem and think flexibly about it. When a problem is written vertically, many students immediately jump to the standard algorithm without giving the problem any thought at all. After writing the problem on the board, I waited for some volunteers.

"You can write the problem vertically," Marshall suggested.

"Yes," I agreed. "I wrote it horizontally, but it could be rewritten vertically."

The students seemed a bit stumped by what to say next.

To further the discussion, I decided to ask some questions that would prompt students to think about the problem in different ways. "Is the answer going to be more or less than one hundred?" I asked.

"Less!" came the reply.

"How do you know?" I asked.

"Because you're subtracting," Dena explained. "Subtraction is taking away. If you start with one hundred and take some away, you're going to have less."

"That makes sense to me," I responded. "Is the answer going to be more or less than fifty? Turn to a partner and see if you can come up with a way to talk about this."

The students talked briefly. Although the question wasn't particularly challenging, I wanted to give them some time to talk about the problem in a way they hadn't before.

Arturo explained, "One hundred minus fifty is fifty. One hundred minus sixty-seven means you're taking away one more ten and seven more ones. So you're going to have less than fifty."

"Ah," I remarked, "you used the benchmark number of fifty. You know what one hundred minus fifty is, so you used that information to help you think about one hundred minus sixty-seven. Did anyone think about it in a different way?"

"I just thought about tens," Ronald shared. "One hundred minus sixty is forty, so I know it's going to be less than fifty."

"OK," I said to the class. "Here's another way for you to think about this problem. Talk to a partner about a story you can make up that goes with the situation. So you need to create a story that goes with one hundred minus sixty-seven."

I gave the students a few minutes to make up their stories. Since they were all seated on the rug, there was a lot of cross-pollination of ideas.

I called on Paulo to share his story.

"I had one hundred candies. I gave sixty-seven to my friends. How many do I have left?"

"Does that story work?" I asked the class. There was consensus that it was fine.

"Any other ideas?" I asked.

"There were one hundred birds. Sixty-seven flew away. How many were left?" Angela offered.

"That works," I acknowledged.

Many students had stories to share, but I didn't want to spend more time on this particular avenue. I had them tell their stories to a partner. This way, all students got a chance to voice their ideas in a minimal amount of time.

"Is there anything else you can tell me about this problem?" I asked.

"I think the answer is going to be in the thirties," Esmirna told us.

"Why do you think that?" I probed.

"Because I know one hundred minus seventy is thirty. And sixty-seven is close to seventy."

"And it's going to end with a three," Patty posited.

"How do you know?" I questioned.

"Because ten minus seven is three," she explained. "If you start at the ones, it will be three."

From here I had the students solve the problem mentally. We had a brief number talk about their strategies. (See "Number Talks" for more details.) I was pleased with this initial *Tell Me All You Can* discussion. I had pushed the students beyond their usual problem-solving process. I knew as this activity was repeated they would become more comfortable with thinking beyond the answer. Ideally, they would get into the habit of thinking about every problem as a whole before they attempted to solve it. This would ensure they would think about reasonableness with flexibility, which would help them both in test-taking situations and in real life.

Extending the Activity

This activity works equally well with any type of number problem. Depending on the current unit of study, choose any operation and whole numbers, fractions, decimals, or percents. The key is communication. As students become accustomed to these types of discussions, they will increase their ability to talk about the problems. Initially, they may get stuck on finding the answer, so it's important to ask leading questions to offer students other ways to think about the equation.

23

CONTENT AREA

Number and
Operations

MATERIALS

- optional: overhead
  projector
- optional: 1–100
  chart

TIME

ten minutes

Twenty Questions

Overview

The game of *Twenty Questions* presents surprising challenges for students. In this guessing game, students generate questions to hone in on a secret number. The act of generating questions requires much thinking and pushes students to consider numbers, how they can be decomposed and recombined, and their connections to real life. Students also develop flexibility in their thinking about numbers as the teacher asks them to create different types of questions. This activity encourages teacher questions and student discussion throughout the experience.

Activity Directions

1. Think of a secret number between 1 and 100.
2. Explain the rules of the game to the students:
   - Tell students that they need to ask yes-or-no questions and that a guess is not considered a question (i.e., "Is the secret number twelve?" is a guess, not a question).
   - Tell students they must ask twenty questions to figure out what the secret number is before they'll be allowed to guess what it is.
3. Have students begin asking questions. Use tallies on the board or an overhead to keep track of the number of questions asked.
4. Stop occasionally to have students discuss what they already know about the secret number and what questions they might ask next.
5. Remind students that when they think they know your secret number, rather than shout it out, they should test it out by asking a good question about the number.
6. After students have asked twenty questions, let them guess the secret number.

Key Questions

- What do you know about the secret number so far?
- How many numbers have you narrowed it down to?
- What types of questions are helpful? Explain.
- What next question can you ask in order to eliminate a lot of possibilities?
- Can you ask a question that connects the secret number to something in real life?

From the Classroom

I introduced the game to a group of third and fourth graders by asking if they were familiar with *Twenty Questions*. Although some students claimed they were, I took a minute to explain the rules.

"I have a secret number and your job is to figure out what it is. There are two important rules: You can only ask me questions about my number that I can answer with yes or no. They have to be real questions about my number, not just a guess. The other rule is that you must ask all twenty questions before you guess my number. So if you think you know what my secret number is, don't shout it out; test it out by asking a smart question."

The students seemed eager to get started. I drew a box with a question mark on the board to give the students a visual reminder that they were trying to solve a mystery.

"OK," I said, "who wants to ask me a question about my secret number?"

Many hands shot into the air. I called on Sofia.

"Is it even?" she asked.

"No," I responded, "my number is not even."

I put a tally mark on the board to keep track of the question and then checked in with the group. "So what do you know about my secret number so far?" I asked.

"It's odd," several students stated immediately.

I concurred and called on Trista.

"Is it above or below fifty?" she asked.

"Hmm," I said, "that's a good question, but I can't answer that with yes or no. Can anyone think of a way to ask the question so I can tell you yes or no?"

The students were stumped. I decided to model a question for them.

"What if you just asked me if it's below fifty? I can tell you yes or no, and then you'll know from my answer whether it's more or less than fifty. Do you want to try that?"

Trista agreed and I told her that yes, my number was below fifty. I then directed the students' attention to the 1–100 chart posted on the wall. This particular chart had even numbers posted in white and odd numbers posted in red.

"Take a look at the one-to-one-hundred chart," I told the students. "Can someone go to the chart and point out where my secret number is on the chart?"

Edward went to the chart and swept his arm across the top half of the chart.

"Right," I agreed, "You know my number is somewhere between one and fifty. What else do you know about my secret number?"

Ivette reminded the group that the number was odd.

"Good," I said. "So if I look at the chart, I see that all the odd numbers are red and that helps me."

I pointed to the vertical stripes of odd numbers between 1 and 50. "It's one of these numbers," I said. "Now who wants to ask me another question?"

"Is it close to forty?" Edward asked.

Again I realized that the students needed help with framing their questions and asking them precisely. With repeated practice students will gain this skill, but when introducing the game, anticipate that you'll need some time to model question forming. Edward's question fit the yes-or-no parameters, but the concept of *close* depends on context and could not be answered definitively.

"That's a tough question for me to answer. How close is *close*? One person might think ten away is close but someone else might think one away is close."

"Is it in the twenties?" Adelia asked.

While Adelia's question moved us away from the close-to-forty issue, I decided to use it as an illustration for the class. I went to the 1–100 chart.

"No," I replied, "it's not in the twenties, so now when I look at the possibilities, I can eliminate this whole row." I pointed to the row of twenties. Subsequently students asked several questions in the same vein.

"Is it in the thirties?"

"Is it in the forties?"

When we had established that my secret number was in the forties, I redirected the students and had them talk to a partner about what types of questions were helpful and what next question they might ask in order to eliminate possibilities. I did this in order to avoid further unnecessary questions about whether my number was in the teens, in the ones, and so on. I wanted to move the students toward a new line of questions. The students focused on odd numbers in the forties and were forced to generate different types of questions.

Ellie asked if my number was more than forty-five. I asked her why she chose forty-five.

"We already know it's in the forties," Ellie explained, "so I went to the middle of the forties to see if it's more or less."

"Well," I responded, "the answer to your question is no. My secret number is not more than forty-five. That information should help you a lot."

I went to the hundreds chart to illustrate how Ellie had eliminated two of the possibilities (47 and 49) with one question.

Trinesha then asked if my number was one away from forty-four. After I told her it was not, Joey asked if my number had a one in it. When I told him it did, I knew it was time to redirect again.

"Nod your head if you're pretty sure you know what my secret number is," I told the class. Almost everyone nodded.

"OK," I reminded them, "the rules for this game are that you have to ask twenty questions before you can guess, so even if you know my number, you need to think of more questions. So far you've asked eight questions. That means you need to ask twelve more before you can guess. Maybe you can ask questions that will test out your idea to make sure you really know the secret number."

I got a new series of questions. "Is it below forty-three?" "Is it below forty-two?" Does it have a four in it?" Clearly the students now knew that my secret number was forty-one, but I wanted to push them to decompose the number and apply some operation sense. I made a suggestion.

"I can tell by your questions that you've figured out my secret number. You still need to ask a few more questions before you can guess. I wonder if you can ask some questions that have addition or subtraction in them. Maybe you can think about what plus what equals my number and ask me questions like that."

I gave the students a moment to think about this new type of question. The wait time paid off. The students did some mental computation and asked some good questions.

"Is it thirty plus eleven?"

"Is it forty plus one?"

"Is it twenty plus twenty-one?"

"Is it forty-three minus one?"

I decided to change directions one more time with the few remaining questions.

"Well," I told the class, "you seem to know my number, but you've still got a couple of questions left. I'm going to give you a minute to quietly talk to a partner about when and where you might find this number in real life."

The students were a bit hesitant but a few examples emerged.

"Could it be someone's age?" Marshall asked.

"Yes," I agreed.

"Is it the number of fingers on four peoples' hands, plus one more finger?" Sofia proposed.

"Yes again," I responded.

The stretching required to ask the questions forced the students to think about numbers in many ways and to make many connections. When the students had finally asked me twenty questions, I allowed them to guess my secret number. Rather than call on one individual, I had the whole class tell me in unison. This way all students got to be "right" and had the opportunity to successfully participate in the activity.

Extending the Activity

The *Twenty Questions* game is really two games in one. At the beginning, students use logical thinking to ask questions that systematically narrow down the possibilities and zero in on the secret number. Somewhere about halfway through the game, students usually have a pretty good idea of what the secret number is. At this point, they need to think about the number in a variety of ways. They start to ask questions about magnitude and begin breaking the number apart in a variety of ways. Prompting from the teacher is essential in helping students form effective and varied questions.

Once students become familiar with the mechanics of the game, they can become the leaders of the game. A student or pair of students can think of a secret number and answer questions from the class. The game can also be focused on specific areas of arithmetic that students need to practice. You can encourage students to ask questions that involve multiplication or properties of the number (odd, even, prime, composite), for example. Students can also use this activity to connect numbers and quantities to real life, thus making math more relevant and accessible.

This activity can also be adapted for geometry. A secret shape can be the focal point and students can ask yes-or-no questions about its properties and uses in real life.

What Comes Next?

24

CONTENT AREA

Algebra

MATERIALS

- optional: overhead projector

TIME

five to ten minutes

Overview

What Comes Next? focuses students' attention on pattern recognition, a foundational idea of algebraic thinking, and mathematical communication. In this activity, the teacher begins a number pattern on the board. The students need to predict the next three numbers in the pattern. Students also need to verbally describe the pattern and justify their predictions using mathematical reasoning. Students are further challenged to find examples of the pattern in the real world.

Activity Directions

1. Begin a number pattern on the board or an overhead (e.g., 2 4 6 __ __ __).
2. Ask students to think about what numbers would come next in the pattern.
3. Have students explain the pattern in as many ways as possible and record their ideas on the board.
4. Ask students to think about where this pattern occurs in real life.
5. Repeat Steps 1 through 4 with a different pattern.

Key Questions

- What is the pattern?
- Is there another way to describe the pattern?
- Can you think of real-life examples of this pattern?

From the Classroom

Melissa Mechtly introduced *What Comes Next?* to her third graders by asking them what they knew about patterns. After establishing their familiarity with the idea, she began the activity.

"So I'm going to start a pattern," Melissa told her class, "and your job is to think about what numbers come next in the pattern. You also need to think about why those numbers come next. When I call on you I'm going to ask you to explain the thinking behind your answer, so be prepared."

It's important to let students know what's expected of them. Since Melissa wanted her students to focus on justifying their answers, she needed to let them know at the outset that they would be asked to do that. Also, she didn't want anyone to feel put on the spot.

She started with a simple pattern.

1 2 3 __ __ __

"That's so easy!" Janet exclaimed.

"Well this is just the warm-up to make sure you understand how the activity works," Melissa responded. "Don't worry. I've got some trickier patterns for you."

"So who thinks you know what the next number is?" Melissa continued.

"Four comes next," John announced.

"How do you know?" Melissa asked.

"Because it's just counting," John explained.

"Counting by what?" Melissa pushed.

"Counting by ones," several students exclaimed.

Melissa wrote on the board:

Counting by 1s

"So if my pattern is counting by ones," she said to her class, "what would come after four?"

"Five!" the students replied with confidence.

"And then?"

"Six!"

Melissa filled in the pattern on the board.

1 2 3 <u>4</u> <u>5</u> <u>6</u>

"Is there another way to describe this pattern?" she asked.

"Plus one," Chantelle suggested.

"Adding one," Rachel contributed.

Melissa wrote these two descriptions on the board. She turned the students' attention to what they had done so far.

1 2 3 <u>4</u> <u>5</u> <u>6</u>　　　*counting by ones*
　　　　　　　　　plus one
　　　　　　　　　adding one

"OK," she said, "you figured out my pattern and have several ways to describe it. Now here's another question for you. Can you think of any examples of this pattern in real life? Talk to a partner and see if you can come up with some places where you find this pattern outside of math class."

Melissa gave the students a minute to talk to each other. She noticed that most of the students were looking around the classroom for ideas and weren't really thinking outside of the school context. She realized she would need to prompt them a bit. She started by taking some of their classroom-based suggestions.

"The number line," Omar pointed out.

"The calendar," Carol added.

"Our table numbers," Vincent said.

"Wow," Melissa responded, "this pattern shows up a lot around here. What about outside our classroom? Can you think of any examples?"

Seeing her students' blank stares, Melissa gave them a hint. "Hakim told me that tomorrow is his birthday. Do birthdays have a pattern?"

"Oh yeah," Joshua said, "first you're one year old, then you're two years old, then you're three years old . . ."

Melissa cut him off well before he reached middle age. "Aha," she said, "so there's another example of this pattern. I bet you'll notice it a lot in your lives once you start thinking about it. Now let's try a trickier pattern." She wrote on the board:

2 4 __ __ __

"That's so easy!" several students blurted out.

"Hang on," Melissa cautioned. "I gave you only two numbers in the pattern. That's not a lot of information. There might be more than one pattern that fits those numbers. Talk to a neighbor and see how many different possibilities you can come up with."

Melissa let the students have a brief discussion. When she was satisfied they had multiple answers and reasons, she called for their attention.

"OK," she said, "who has an idea about what might come next in this pattern? Remember you also need to tell why that number comes next."

"It could be six," Liliana suggested.

"And why could it be six?" Melissa probed.

"Because it's counting by twos," Liliana explained.

"All right," Melissa responded. "If that's the pattern, what would come next?"

"Eight!" shouted the class.

"Right," Melissa agreed. "Did anyone come up with another possibility?"

"It could be two," Chantelle announced.

"How would that work?" the teacher asked.

"Because," Chantelle explained, "the pattern could be two, four, two, four, two, four."

"Oh," Melissa replied. "It could be a repeating pattern instead of a growing pattern. I'll tell you that this particular pattern is a growth pattern. So if you know that it's a growth pattern, are there any other possibilities?"

"Maybe eight," Katy offered.

"Why eight?" Melissa asked.

"It could be like two times two is four and four times two is eight."

"I see," Melissa said, "so it might be a multiply-by-two, or a doubling, pattern. If it's a doubling pattern, what would come next? Talk to a partner about the next few numbers in Katy's pattern."

Melissa let the students work through the computation and then they added the next four numbers to the pattern.

2 4 8 16 32 64

"Wow," Melissa exclaimed. "Those numbers get big pretty fast. So now here's my next question: When does this pattern occur in real life? Talk to your neighbors and see if you can come up with anything."

Melissa gave the students some time to discuss the pattern. As she listened to their discussions, she realized they had a hard time distinguishing this doubling pattern from a multiples-of-two pattern. This point is confusing since both patterns rely on multiplying by two. However, multiples of two increase by only two each time (e.g., two, four, six, eight, . . .). The doubling pattern Melissa presented involves powers of two that cause the numbers to increase exponentially. She decided she needed to show the students an example. She took a piece of blank paper and held it up.

"How many rectangles do I have?" she asked the class.

"One," the class responded.

"OK," Melissa told them, "I'm going to fold the paper in half. Then how many rectangles will I have when I open it back up?"

"Two," the students replied.

Melissa folded the paper in half and opened it to confirm their prediction. "So what will happen if I fold it in half and then in half again?" she continued.

The students responded, "Four."

Melissa continued the folding process, asking the students each time how many rectangles there would be. The students soon caught on to the connection between the paper folding and the pattern on the board. They were fascinated and wanted to see how many times their teacher could actually fold the paper. She indulged them, finally stopping when she had created thirty-two little rectangles.

"Actually," she pointed out to the class, "I think this pattern starts with one, not two. Let me write that and see if the pattern still works."

1 2 4 8 16 32

"Does this show what happened when I folded the paper? Is it still a doubling pattern?"

The class agreed that it did represent the folded paper. Melissa told them that this pattern occurred a lot in mathematical and scientific situations. She also told them it was called *powers of two*. She didn't think it was necessary to go into a long explanation of exponents and exponential growth. She just wanted to make them aware of this important pattern. She encouraged the children to look for this pattern in the real world and come back to share what they discovered.

Extending the Activity

What Comes Next? works well as a review of multiplication facts. Start with any number and give its subsequent multiples (e.g., 3 6 9 __ __ __). The activity can also be used to introduce mathematical patterns such as square numbers, triangle numbers (1 3 6 10 __ __ __), and a common pattern in nature, Fibonacci numbers (0 1 1 2 3 5 8 __ __ __). Students can also create their own number patterns and have the class guess what comes next and how the patterns work.

25

What Page Are We On?

CONTENT AREA

Number and
Operations

Data Analysis and
Probability

MATERIALS

- a book
- a bookmark
- optional: overhead
  projector

TIME

five to ten minutes

Overview

Often, the upper-elementary day includes a time when the teacher reads a chapter book aloud to the class. The chapter book read-aloud gives the teacher an opportunity to engage children's number sense with a quick question: "What page do you think we're on?" This question prompts students to estimate and perform some mental computation.

Number sense plays a key role in children's mathematical development. Students need many opportunities with estimation and mental computation. They also need much exposure to a variety of strategies and methods. Leading short discussions with a real-world context, such as estimating the page number the class is on in a read-aloud book, accomplishes two important goals. First, students become more flexible in their thinking about numbers and their connections to the real world. Second, over time students hear many different ideas about numbers and operations that help them build their own arsenal of problem-solving strategies.

Activity Directions

1. Hold up a book with a bookmark in it so that students can see where the bookmark is placed relative to the entire thickness of the book.
2. Ask students to estimate the number of pages in the book. Record their estimates on the board or an overhead.
3. Help the students determine the range of their estimates. Have students share their computation strategies and record them on the board.
4. Reveal the number of pages in the book.
5. Ask students to estimate what page the bookmark is on.
6. Lead a brief discussion about the students' estimates that focuses on number sense and different approaches to solving the problem.
7. Reveal the page the bookmark is on.

Key Questions

- About how many pages do you think this book has? Can you explain your thinking?
- About what fraction of the book have we read so far?
- Did anyone get the same answer using a different method?
- Did anyone come up with a different estimate or think about the problem in a different way?

From the Classroom

I began by asking a mixed group of third- through fifth-grade students if they were familiar with the book *Holes,* by Louis Sachar. Students told me that they had read the book, seen the movie, and heard the rap song. I didn't know there was a rap song, but when they started singing it, I told them I believed them.

I held up a copy of *Holes* with a bookmark marking my place. I continued the session by asking the students to estimate how many pages they thought were in the book. I asked them to each think of their estimate and raise their hand when they were ready to share it. Then I did a "lightning round," quickly pointing to a student, having the student say the estimate, and writing the number on the board. In less than a minute the board was full of estimates.

215	300	320
260	150	195
250	180	369
290	210	190

I decided to gather a bunch of estimates first without stopping to discuss individuals' thinking. My goal was to encourage all students to offer an estimate without pressure. I also wanted to collect a range of numbers on the board for us to analyze.

"Let's find the range of your estimates," I suggested to the class.

Noticing the puzzled looks, I decided to scaffold this task a bit more. I explained, "The first step to finding the range is to look at all the numbers up here and find the lowest and the highest. Take a minute to find those two numbers."

It didn't take long for students to identify 150 as the lowest estimate and 369 as the highest. I circled those two numbers on the board. I continued, "The next step to finding the range is to figure the difference between one hundred fifty and three hundred sixty-nine."

I gave the students a few minutes to discuss this with a partner. Then I had a several students share their thinking.

"I lined up the numbers up and down in my head," Aimee explained. "Then I just did the subtraction in my head."

I wrote on the board:

$$\begin{array}{r} 369 \\ -\ 150 \\ \hline \end{array}$$

"So you used the mental chalkboard strategy," I summarized. "Did you start with the ones or the hundreds?"

Although I was pretty sure Aimee had used the traditional algorithm, starting in the ones column, I wanted to publicize the possibility that there were other ways to deal with the computation.

"I started with the ones," Aimee confirmed. "I got two hundred nineteen."

I completed Aimee's solution on the board:

$$\begin{array}{r} 369 \\ -\ 150 \\ \hline 219 \end{array}$$

"Did anyone get the same answer using a different method?" I asked.

Marco shared his solution. "I added one hundred to one hundred fifty, and that got me to two hundred fifty. Then I added another one hundred to get to three fifty. Then I added a ten and a nine and that made three sixty-nine."

I decided an open number line would be an effective tool for helping students visualize what Marco had done.

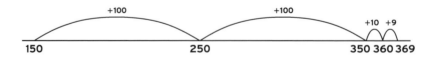

"So you added one hundred plus one hundred plus ten plus nine, which equals two hundred nineteen," I said, pointing to the number line. "You did get the same answer as Aimee. So it looks like there's agreement that the range of your estimates is two hundred nineteen."

I moved along. "OK, I'm going to tell you that you did a nice job with your estimates. I'm thinking that because the actual number of pages in the book is in the middle of your estimates. The book actually has two hundred thirty-three pages."

I gave the students a moment to digest this exciting information. Then I showed them the bookmark that was sticking out of the top of the book again. I gave the students a view of the top of the book so they could see the bookmark and its position relative to the thickness of the book.

"So you now know there are two hundred thirty-three pages in the whole book," I reminded the students. "With that in mind, what page of the book do you think I'm on right now? You can see where the bookmark is to help you. I'd like to hear some ideas about your estimates. Then you can make some estimates and I'll write them on the board."

"It looks like the bookmark is about halfway," Aja observed.

"More like eight-twelfths," countered Christian.

"Fractions can help you think about your estimates," I validated. "What else can you do to help you estimate what page I'm on?"

"If we know there are two hundred thirty-three pages, then we know the page we're on is going to be about half of that or a little more than half," Devin offered.

"Well, I've read that book already," Maddy stated. "I'm pretty sure there are thirty-five chapters. So I can guess you're on about Chapter Twenty."

"That could help," I commented. "So talk to a partner about your estimate for what page we're on. Also, make sure you discuss your reasoning so your partner understands how you got your idea."

I gave the students a couple of minutes to talk. As they talked, I circulated, showing them the book and the bookmark. Occasionally, I'd ask students to remind me how many total pages there were in the book. This question helped them focus on reasonableness. In a short while I called for the class's attention and then had students share their estimates and their rationales for those estimates. Many students used the benchmark of one-half to estimate.

"I think you're on page one hundred sixteen because one hundred sixteen plus one hundred sixteen is two hundred thirty-two, and that's practically two hundred thirty-three," Thea explained.

"My estimate is one twenty-five because it looks like it's a little more than half," Reggie volunteered.

After listening to a few more students, I told the class that the bookmark was actually on page 131. I asked students to each mentally calculate the difference between their estimate and the actual page number. They shared that information with their partners. I encouraged them to use the strategies suggested for estimating in the future when I came back to ask them what page they were on in another book.

Extending the Activity

Using books as an estimating activity opens many possibilities. The same question can be revisited over time during the course of a read-aloud. Flip the question by telling students what page you're on and asking them to estimate how many pages are in the entire book. Also, books can be compared with each other. Hold up two books and ask, "If the book in my right hand has two hundred fifteen pages, about how many pages do you think this other book has?" In addition, you can incorporate the element of time by asking such questions as, "The book we're reading has one hundred seventy-nine pages. Today we read twenty-one pages. About how many days do you think it will take to finish the whole book?"

Gathering the estimates on sticky notes and posting them on the board also gives a context for data analysis. Students can find the range, mode, and median of their estimates (see "Looking at Data" for more details).

Whole-Class Pig

26

Overview

The game of pig is a popular probability game usually played by partners or in small groups. In this version of the game, the whole class participates together, making it a quicker, yet equally engaging activity.

Probability games, especially those involving dice and cards, supply absorbing occasions for strategic thinking and arithmetic practice in context. This game gets students to consider likely and unlikely outcomes while practicing addition. It's also nice because it gets students up on their feet and moving around a bit.

Activity Directions

1. Ask the students to stand up by their desks.
2. To begin a round of *Whole-Class Pig*, the teacher rolls two dice and tells students the number on each die. The students state the sum aloud.
3. Each student writes the sum on his or her paper.
4. Each student decides whether to save the points earned from that roll or to keep going. If a student decides to save his or her points, he or she circles the total and turns the paper over. The student also sits down until the end of the round.
5. The round continues until all students have sat down and flipped their papers over or until a 1 appears on a roll.
6. If a 1 appears on either die, students who did not save their points lose all the points they accumulated on that round.
7. If two 1s appear on the dice, everyone goes back to zero, regardless of how many points he or she saved on the previous rounds.
8. The goal is to get 100 points. It's OK to go over 100. As soon as a student reaches or surpasses 100, he or she should raise a hand.
9. Lead a discussion for students to share their strategies and to consider if some sums are more likely than others.

CONTENT AREA

Data Analysis and
Probability

Number and Operations

MATERIALS

■ 2 dice

TIME

ten to fifteen minutes

Key Questions

- What strategy are you using?
- How did you decide when to stop?
- Are some rolls more likely than others?

From the Classroom

Rather than starting with a lengthy explanation, I decided to jump right into the game *Whole-Class Pig* with Olivia Gonzalez's fifth graders. The students would need to ask me questions about the rules as they arose. I asked all the students to stand up, push their chairs in, and stand in front of their desks.

"OK," I began, "each of you has a piece of paper and a pencil. I'm going to roll these two dice and the sum of the dice is your score. Are you ready?"

I checked and noted the nodding heads and smiles. I rolled the dice.

"It's a five and a three. What's the total?" I asked. I always tell the amount on each die and have the students do the addition. I try to capitalize on any occasion for students to practice basic facts or do arithmetic in context.

"Eight," came the unanimous response.

"Good," I said, "so now everyone has eight points. Write an *eight* on your paper. If you want to save your points, circle the eight, flip your paper over, and sit down. If you want to keep going, just remain standing and leave the eight faceup."

I looked around the room and noticed some puzzled faces. I plowed on, hoping someone would stop me and ask for clarification.

"So, I'm looking around the room and some of you have flipped your papers over and sat down, which means you're stopping, but most of you haven't. I'm going to roll again and those of you who are still standing can add the next roll to your total."

"That's not fair!" argued Andi, who had flipped her paper over and was sitting down.

"Why not?" I queried.

"Because some people will keep getting points and we'll be stuck with eight."

"Aha," I replied, "I need to explain one other rule to this game. If you decide to keep going and I roll a one on either die, you lose all the points for this round."

"What if we did circle our eight and sat down?" Daniel asked.

"Then your points are safe and you can't lose them," I explained. "There's one other rule you need to know. If I roll double ones, or snake eyes, you lose all your points, even the ones you saved. Everyone goes all the way back to zero. So let's hope that doesn't happen."

It was my hope that students would take ownership of the game and assert themselves. I wanted them to realize there was information missing and that they needed to ask questions in order to find out the details they lacked. I don't always want to spoon-feed everything to the students. They need to take charge of their learning and begin to insist that things make sense before they proceed. Introducing the *Whole-Class Pig* game in general terms forced the students to make sense of it and ask questions when they needed more information. I had the students turn to their partners and tell the rules as they understood them. After this brief interlude I continued with the game. I rolled a 1 and a 3.

"Uh oh," I told the class, "I just rolled a one and a three. So what does that mean?"

"We're back to zero," Edgardo proclaimed glumly.

"No," Keenan argued, "not if we saved our points."

"That's right," I agreed. "If you flipped your paper over and sat down, you still have eight points. If you kept going, you're now at zero. So right now everyone either has eight points or zero points. Everyone stand up and flip your papers back up and we're going to play Round Two."

"What are we trying to do?" Tina asked.

"Another great question," I replied. "The goal of this game is to get one hundred points. So you always have the choice of saving the points you have or continuing on for more points in each round. The only problem is that if you decide to be a pig and go for more points, you might end up losing all your points. That's why this game is called *Whole-Class Pig*."

I rolled again and students recorded their new totals on their papers. After each roll I asked students to either circle their new totals, sit down, and flip their papers or hang in and continue. Each round ended either with a roll of 1 or all students saving their points. Then we started a new round. After several rounds I polled the students about their current totals.

"Does anyone have more than twenty?" I asked.

I deliberately started with a low number that I knew everyone in the class had surpassed. That way, all students would feel some success and be able to raise their hands.

"How about more than thirty?" I continued.

I saw fewer hands this time.

"Wait," exclaimed Umberto, "I'm not sure what I have."

"Let's see if the class can help," I offered.

Umberto told me his total points from each round and I wrote them on the board. I gave the students a few moments to find the sum of Umberto's number string (see "Number Strings" for more details).

Umberto's Points

14 + 10 + 4 + 4 + 11 =

An opening for a quick number talk arose, and I took advantage. I had several students share their thinking. I began with Umberto since it was his score we were talking about. He had just added the numbers from left to right. Other students started with the tens or saw a lot of fours and grouped them together first. After establishing Umberto's total and acknowledging the various ways to compute it, we got back to the game.

"Is this like bingo?" David asked.

"I'm not sure I know what you mean," I told him.

"Like, if we get one hundred, do we yell something out?" he clarified.

"Hmm," I said, "I guess when you get to one hundred, you can raise your hand."

"Does it have to be exactly one hundred?" Shante asked.

"Another good question," I responded. "You don't need to get exactly one hundred. You can go over."

We continued the game. I rolled the two dice, told the students the results, and had them say the sum aloud each time. This game really allowed the students' individual personalities to shine. Some students boldly remained standing through many rolls. Other students took a conservative approach and proudly circled and saved their points after one or two rolls. Others showed more hesitancy and looked to their friends for cues. Throughout the game there was a good deal of talking, laughing, and interaction. I established a signal so the students would settle down and focus before each new roll. I told the students I would count down from three, at which point I expected them to either be standing or sitting. Also they all needed to be quietly paying attention to the upcoming roll. This approach worked well. It allowed the children to express their enthusiasm while allowing me to manage the group and keep the activity moving.

We continued playing until several students announced they had reached 100. At this point we stopped the game and had a brief discussion.

"I'm curious to know if any of you had a strategy or plan while we were playing," I prompted the class.

"I think it's good to take a risk and keep going," Katy shared.

"I stopped after two or three or four rolls," Henry stated.

"How did you decide when to stop?" I pushed.

"Well," Henry explained, "if you rolled some high numbers like fives or sixes, then I would stop sooner to save my points. If you rolled low numbers I would keep going because I didn't have much to lose."

"Interesting strategy," I acknowledged. "Other people might want to try that strategy the next time we play."

Then I shifted the focus of the discussion. "This game involves probability," I explained to the class. "When I roll the dice we don't know exactly what is going to happen, but there might be some outcomes that are more likely and some that are unlikely. Did anyone notice sums that seemed more likely to occur? Were there certain numbers that came up more than other numbers?"

I deliberately asked the same question in two ways to help students connect the mathematical vocabulary with familiar words and concepts.

"It seemed like you rolled a lot of eights," Martin observed.

"So eight is a more likely sum when I roll the dice?" I inserted appropriate vocabulary as I restated Martin's idea.

"Yes," Martin agreed.

"Can anyone tell a sum that seemed unlikely? Something that hardly happened at all?"

"You never got double ones," Cindy responded.

"Lucky for us!" Angela added.

"So it seems unlikely that double ones will occur when I roll the dice," I restated. "Is it possible to get double ones?"

"Yes!" was the resounding response.

"Sure," I agreed, "it's possible that it could happen, but it's unlikely. When I visit again we can explore some of these probability ideas further. Maybe that will help you think about other strategies for the game of *Whole-Class Pig*."

Extending the Activity

Playing *Whole-Class Pig* with the class is lively and engaging. Once students have played the game a few times and discussed likely and unlikely sums, lead some other probability investigations. One easy way to look more deeply at the probability aspect of the game is to graph the sums as they are rolled. Display a class graph and add to it over time. Simple tally marks next to each sum rolled will soon reveal likely and unlikely sums.

2	‖
3	ǀ
4	‖|
5	‖‖
6	‖|
7	卌 ǀ
8	卌 ‖
9	‖|
10	‖‖
11	ǀ
12	‖

If students play the game with partners, they can keep track of the sums rolled and add the data to the class graph. With enough data the graph will begin to resemble the famous bell-shaped curve. The graph can be used as a jumping-off point for a discussion about game strategy and how it relates to the data posted. A further investigation involves determining all the possible two-dice combinations and relating that information to the graph and the game.

Another version of the game involves playing ten rounds of pig. The goal is for students to see how many points they can get in those ten rounds. They may reach or surpass 100, but that isn't the focus. In some ways this version mitigates the competitive race to be the first to get to 100. Instead all students are testing out their strategies to see how well they work.

Your Choice Tic-Tac-Toe

27

Overview

Your Choice Tic-Tac-Toe offers a new twist to the traditional tic-tac-toe game. The goal remains the same—get three in a row—but on each turn the student may choose to be either an X or an O. While challenging students to break the old habit of remaining either X or O for the entire game, *Your Choice Tic-Tac-Toe* also provides opportunities for spatial reasoning and strategy development.

Activity Directions

1. Explain to students that *Your Choice Tic-Tac-Toe* is just like regular tic-tac-toe with one twist: players may choose whether to be X or O on each turn instead of keeping one symbol or the other for the entire game.
2. To demonstrate for the entire class how to play the game, ask two student volunteers to play a game as you guide them.
3. Draw a tic-tac-toe game board on the board or an overhead.
4. Player A puts either an X or an O anywhere on the game board.
5. Player B puts either an X or an O anywhere on the board.
6. Play continues until one player completes a line of three in a row.
7. Ask another pair to play a game in front of the class.
8. Have students play the game in pairs.
9. Lead a discussion for students to share their opinions of game and discoveries they made about *Your Choice Tic-Tac-Toe*.

Key Questions

- What did you think of this game?
- What discoveries did you make?

CONTENT AREA

Geometry

MATERIALS

- optional: overhead projector

TIME

ten to fifteen minutes

From the Classroom

"Raise your hand if you know how to play tic-tac-toe," I said to Melissa Mechtly's third graders.

Hands shot into the air along with a murmur of excitement.

"Well," I continued, "today you're going to learn a new version of tic-tac-toe. It's the same as regular tic-tac-toe in a lot of ways. You use the same board. You play with a partner. You use Xs and Os. You want to get three in a row horizontally, vertically, or diagonally. But there's one big difference." I wrote on the board:

Your Choice Tic-Tac-Toe

"In *Your Choice Tic-Tac-Toe*, you get to decide whether you want to use an X or an O on every turn. With regular tic-tac-toe you pick which partner is X and which is O at the beginning of the game and you stick with it. This version of the game gives you the choice of changing your symbol on each turn."

"Huh?" Charlie responded.

"Yeah," Kayla agreed, "I don't get it."

I wasn't surprised at the students' confusion. Mere verbal directions often leave questions and uncertainties. I wanted to give the students a brief overview of the game and connect it to a game they already knew. However, I would need to model a game in front of the whole class to help the students really understand.

"How about this?" I suggested to the class. "Let's get two volunteers up here to play a game of *Your Choice Tic-Tac-Toe*. That way everyone can see what the game looks like and ask questions about it."

Hands flew into the air as almost all students wanted to play in front of the class. I picked Aisha and Emilio to play a game. I drew a tic-tac-toe grid on the whiteboard and handed each student a marker. Emilio put an O in the upper right corner. Aisha put an X in the middle. Emilio put an O in the upper left corner. Aisha put an O in the top middle box and had three Os in a row. Emilio laughed and slapped his head as he realized his mistake.

"This is tricky," I said. "Sometimes we're so used to doing things a certain way that we forget the rules have changed. Does anyone else want to come up here and play a game in front of the class?"

I called on another boy and girl to play. I try to be aware of gender as I seek volunteers for whole-class activities. Often boys dominate discussions during math time, but it's possible to equalize participation with some deliberate awareness.

The second game was a bit longer since the students had some experience to draw from. They began to see the considerations necessary for this new version of the game. After the game was over, I sent students off to play in pairs. I told them we'd get back together in a few minutes to discuss what they had noticed and learned.

I circulated among the pairs as they played. Typically, students began by forgetting the new rules and making some quick game-ending errors. After a few tries, however, the students began to think more strategically and plan for the possibility of their partners switching from Os to Xs or vice versa. After a while I called the students back to the rug and we discussed their experiences. I started with a very general question to get the conversation going.

"So what do you think of this game?" I asked.

"It's fun," Antoinette replied.

"It's tricky because I kept forgetting that my partner could switch and he kept getting three in a row," Javier added.

"I liked it because I like tic-tac-toe," Carol shared.

"OK," I moved on, "I know you didn't have a lot of time to play, but did you discover anything in the time you had?"

"I made a discovery," Jon announced. "It's good to put an X or an O in the middle. Then if your partner puts the same thing anywhere you can win."

I drew a tic-tac-toe grid and modeled Jon's discovery. Several other students had used the same strategy so there was a consensus about his approach. Students also realized that if both partners knew about this strategy, it would be more difficult to win with it.

"I noticed something else," Hakim added. "If you start with an O in the middle and then you have Xs on the two diagonal corners of the O, you will always win."

"Hmm," I said, "let's take a look at Hakim's idea."

I drew another tic-tac-toe board and had Hakim tell me where to put the Xs and the O.

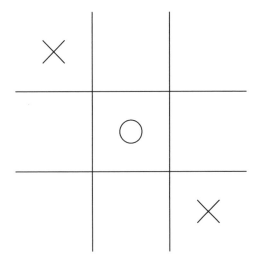

We checked each empty square to see what Hakim would do if his partner put an X or an O in it. Sure enough, Hakim could get three in a row regardless of what his partner did.

"Interesting," I commented. "It seems like there are some good strategies for *Your Choice Tic-Tac-Toe*. When you play again, try out some of these ideas and also see if you can find some other ways to get three in a row."

I left the class, telling the students that I was looking forward to hearing more about their discoveries when I returned.

Extending the Activity

Rather than start with verbal directions, another option is to jump in and model a game with minimal introduction. Then have students generate a list of how regular tic-tac-toe and *Your Choice Tic-Tac-Toe* are the same and different. A Venn diagram or T-chart would serve well as a graphic organizer for the same-different comparisons.

Writing also works well as a follow-up to this activity. Challenge students to write directions for the game. They can also write about their discoveries or strategies. Sentence frames such as "I liked . . . ," "I noticed . . . ," "I discovered . . . ," and "I wonder . . ." help students verbalize their ideas and communicate them in written form.

Your Choice Tic-Tac-Toe also makes a nice homework assignment. Have students teach the game to people at home, play with them, and report or write about the experience.

Blackline Masters

Coordinate Tic-Tac-Toe Grid
Dot Clusters Overhead Transparency
Dot Clusters Recording Sheet

Coordinate Tic-Tac-Toe

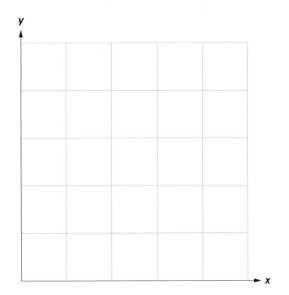

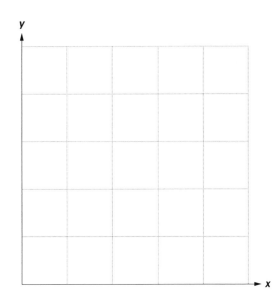

From *Minilessons for Math Practice, Grades 3–5* by Rusty Bresser and Caren Holtzman. © 2006 Math Solutions Publications.

Dot Clusters

Dot Clusters

Index

addition and subtraction
  in benchmark number
    activities, 75–80, 87–91
  effect of patterns and number
    combinations on (activity),
    92–96
  with Function Machine
    (activity), 61–62
  mental math dice activity of
    generating numbers, 13–17
  mental problem-solving and
    discussion activity, 1–6
  in Number Strings (activity),
    87–91
  probability game with addition,
    135–40
  target number game using,
    111–15
algebra
  coordinate graphs, tic-tac-toe
    game with, 30–34
  counting game with strategy
    and logical thinking, 107–10
  Function Machine (activity),
    57–63
associative property, 16–17

Ballpark Estimation (activity),
  7–12
benchmark numbers, 87, 118
  100 (activities), exploring
    numbers' relationship to,
    75–80, 88–91
  defined, 77, 98–99

estimating with (activities),
  7–12, 97–101
  introducing the term, 9
biggest. *See* largest/smallest
Blackline Masters, 145–49
  Coordinate Tic-Tac-Toe
    (game), 147
  Dot Clusters (activity), 148–49
books, in estimating activities,
  130–34

cardinal numbers, 105
chapter book read-aloud, 134
choral response approach, 2–3
classifying numbers by attributes
  (activity), 69–74
Clear the Board (activity), 13–17
Coin Riddle (activity), 18–23
Comparing Fractions (activity),
  24–29
comparison of fractions (activity),
  24–29
compensation, 87
Contents Chart, xv
coordinate graphs, 31–32
  negative numbers, activity
    with, 34
  in tic-tac-toe game context
    (activity), 30–34
Coordinate Tic-Tac-Toe (game),
  30–34
  Blackline Master, 147
counting game with strategy and
  logical thinking, 107–10

data analysis
  graphing activity, 81–86
  with probability game, 135–40
decimals, comparison activity, 29
decomposing numbers, with
  Twenty Questions game,
  120–24
dice
  benchmark number activity
    using, 75–80
  fraction construction using,
    24–29
  mental math computation
    activity with, 13–17
  with probability game, 135–40
  target number addition and
    subtraction game using,
    111–15
Digit Place (game/activity), 35–40
division, mental math dice
  activity of generating
  numbers, 13–17
Dot Clusters (activity), 41–47
  Blackline Masters, 148–49
doubling patterns, 128

equations, activity to explore,
  116–19
estimation
  with benchmark numbers,
    7–12, 97–101
  classroom items, relating to
    (activities), 7–12, 97–101
  defining, 8–9